Shared Wisdom

"Without counsel, plans go wrong, but with many
advisers they succeed." (Proverbs 15:22)

"Without counsel, plans go wrong, but with many advisers they succeed." (Proverbs 15:22)

Shared
Wisdom

A Guide to Case Study
Reflection in Ministry

Jeffrey H. Mahan

Barbara B. Troxell

Carol J. Allen

Abingdon Press
Nashville

SHARED WISDOM: A GUIDE TO CASE STUDY REFLECTION IN MINISTRY

Copyright © 1993 by Abingdon Press

This book is printed on acid-free recycled paper.

Library of Congress Cataloging–in–Publication Data

Mahan, Jeffrey H.
  Shared wisdom : a guide to case study reflection in ministry / Jeffrey H. Mahan, Barbara B. Troxell, Carol J. Allen.
    p.   cm.
  ISBN 0-687-38335-8 (pbk. : alk. paper)
  1. Pastoral theology—Case studies. 2. Seminarians—Case studies. 3. Clergy—Case studies. I. Troxell, Barbara B., 1935–   . II. Allen, Carol J., 1940–   . III. Title.
BV4011.M35 1993
253'.0722—dc20

                                                            93-4458
                                                            CIP

Scripture quotations, except for brief paraphrases or unless otherwise noted, are from the New Revised Standard Version Bible, Copyright 1989 by the Division of Christian Education of the National Council of the Churches of Christ in the USA. Used by permission.

01 02—10 9 8 7 6

MANUFACTURED IN THE UNITED STATES OF AMERICA

PREFACE

Ministry is enriched when its practitioners are involved in a serious process of peer reflection on their ministry. Case study, the method advocated here, is one significant way for such reflection to take place. The discipline of writing an account of some incident in our ministry, of offering up our own analysis of that incident to trusted peers, and then listening to their reflections is particularly valuable in encouraging a reflective practice of ministry.

This book grew out of our work with the Field Education Program at Garrett-Evangelical Theological Seminary (G-ETS). The case-based method of reflection described here is practiced in that program. Between us we bring a range of other experience, including service at other seminaries, in the parish, and at social service agencies. In our own ministries we find that such peer reflection clarifies our self-understanding, our theology and ideology, and our ability to see clearly and empathetically the situations of those with whom we are in ministry. We use it with the faculty and clergy colleagues with whom we supervise students, as well as with the students. We commend it to others for the enrichment of both those now beginning ministry and those whose ministries are based on years of experience.

We offer these ideas, stories, and methodologies with a deep sense of gratitude to those from whom we have learned. We express our particular thanks to the authors of the cases included here, which appear with only very minimal editing, and to the peer groups whose discussions provided the basis for the discussion sections presented here. In order to protect confidentiality, we have changed the names of presenters, participants, and the people and places in the cases. For that reason their names do not appear here. Three colleagues, better able to reflect on how this material could be used in off-campus settings, made contributions to appendix 3. We are grateful for the generosity of George Fitchett, Director of Research and Spiritual Assessment at Rush-Presbyterian-St. Luke's Medical Center, Chicago; Donald Guest, Pastor of Gammon United Methodist Church, Chicago; and Diane Olson, Diaconal Minister of Christian Education at Trinity United Methodist Church in Wilmette, Illinois.

We are deeply appreciative of the work of our colleagues in the Association of Theological Field Education. Our own reflection and practice of the ministry of field education has been challenged and strengthened by our conversations with our colleagues in ATFE and in the Chicago Area Association of Theological Field Education. We also express appreciation to Bob and Alice Evans, Co-Executive Directors of the Association for Case Teaching, and to the participants in A.C.T. Summer Institutes for all they have contributed to our understanding of the case method in teaching in the church. Lynn Rhodes, Associate Professor of Ministry and Field Education at Pacific School of Religion, read an earlier draft of the manuscript and provided commentary which helped us shape the book.

We wish also to thank all the students, faculty, and

field education staff whose words do not appear here, but who have worked with us at G-ETS. We owe a great debt to those who shaped a fine field education program at G-ETS before we arrived. We are particularly aware of the contributions of Douglas Wingeier, Carol Jennings, James Babbitt, and Alvin Lindgren. Our G-ETS colleague Jack Seymour particularly encouraged our work, reading and responding to several generations of the manuscript for this book. Our reflection on the parable of the sower in chapter 3 was guided by the suggestions of one of our site supervisors, Louise Mahan. The image of the prophet Nathan's confrontation with King David as a model for case reflection grew out of conversation with our G-ETS colleague, Peter T. Nash. We express our gratitude to him.

President Neal F. Fisher and Dean Richard D. Tholin made their own and the seminary's support tangible with a grant through the Ministerial Education Fund of The United Methodist Church that supported our research and writing. Judy Russell leapt in, late in the process, to help with word processing. Finally, neither our lives nor this book would be so well focused and organized as they are without the care of our colleague in ministry and program secretary, Otis Thompson.

Jeffrey H. Mahan
Barbara B. Troxell
Carol J. Allen

CONTENTS

Contents

INTRODUCTION

An experienced chaplain and supervisor finds his
personal and professional understandings and
commitments called into question by the challenge of a seminarian doing her field work under his
supervision. A pastor ponders his role as he sits with the
body of a person he has never met and awaits the
arrival of the family to make funeral arrangements. A
Korean woman is presented a cash gift by the grateful
women in the ecumenical and intercultural Bible study
she leads. A newly arrived seminary intern struggles to
set limits in an area where she perceives that she has
more gifts than her supervisor. A youth pastor confronts his own anger and authority when confronted by
the "wrath of mom." Each of these incidents left the
one in ministry feeling alone, dissatisfied with his or
her response, and uncertain about the full implications
of what had happened. They were not, in most cases,
crisis situations, but they raised questions about the
nature and practice of ministry. Situations similar to
these confront every person in ministry and trouble
every thinking minister. Instead of letting the problem
or difficulty overwhelm them, however, the ministers in
the situations just outlined sought out the help of
trusted peers in a process of case reflection designed to
help them learn from the incident. Doing so allowed

them to return to their ministry settings better prepared to reengage the issues and opportunities awaiting them.

This book is offered as an invitation to those involved in ministry—whether in congregations or in specialized settings—to engage in a process of reflection on their practice of ministry. Though our thinking is most directly informed by our work with seminary students reflecting on their experiences in field education, the book is appropriate to anyone in ministry who is willing to understand herself or himself as a learner. This method of learning through reflection calls for a group of people consulting together in a disciplined way on a specific incident in the ministry of one member of the group, who has presented for discussion a brief written account or case. What follows is an explanation of how we understand ministry, and why we think small-group case reflection enriches our practice of ministry.

EACH ONE A MINISTER

We use the familiar term *ministry* in its broad ecclesiastical sense to include all acts of service and proclamation, emerging from the love of God as known in Jesus Christ. We believe that reflection on critical incidents in life is helpful for all people of God. All are called to witness and to service, to worship and to mission in God's world. As the Consultation on Church Union states, "In all its forms and functions, ministry is a rich interweaving of word and worship, work and witness. In different ways, members of the body share responsibility for the Church's government, administration, discipline, instruction, worship, and pastoral care."[1]

---

1. *COCU Consensus: In Quest of a Church of Christ Uniting* (Princeton, N.J.: COCU, 1985), p. 41.

As we share in such responsibility and reach out in service, we, laity and clergy alike, grow through mutual reflection on our experience. Though the majority of readers of this book may well be professionals in the church—either lay or ordained—it is our intent wherever we write "ministry" to include the serving acts of the whole people of God, whether as individuals, a local community, or the church universal. When we refer to those whose primary employment is in ministry, we will write "professional ministry." When we refer specifically to persons ordained to the ministry of word, sacrament, and order, or consecrated to the diaconal ministry of service, justice, and love, we will indicate our intent with a further adjective, such as "ordained" or "consecrated" to modify "ministry." This distinction is not trivial. It reminds us that the ministry of the ordained happens as part of the ministries of the whole people of God. It also helps to make clear that the invitation to theological reflection on their serving is extended to all God's people.

CASE STUDY IS EFFECTIVE

In case study someone in ministry shares a written account of a significant incident in her, or his, ministry with a small group of trusted colleagues for the purpose of theological reflection. With the help of a designated facilitator, members of the group share their analysis and interpretation of the case and the case presenter's actions. Though we are always co-learners, the primary goal of the group is to deepen the presenter's self-understanding, to sharpen his or her clarity about the forces which shape the situation of ministry, and to increase the presenter's effectiveness when he, or she, returns to the ministry site. When each participant

13

takes a turn presenting, mutuality and trust are encouraged.

As a form of collaborative learning, case study contributes to enhancing discipleship. It takes place in small groups of persons who work together to form learning communities in which knowledge arises out of dialogue. Information is not simply transmitted by experts to novices. Room is made for diversity and disagreement. Mutual respect and cooperation are two of the ethical norms in these groups.

Such reflection on practice provides a disciplined structure for ministerial reflection, which enables professional growth and development. The discipline of writing a case requires us as presenters to recognize, describe in detail, and reflect on a particular incident in our own ministry. This specificity seems to open greater possibilities for self-discovery and potential for growth than do more general discussions of "issues" in ministry. The structured process of case study assumes the value of shared reflection and encourages participants to be more disciplined in consultation. The process invites us to acknowledge that we bring our own experiences of ministry and professional identity to our reflection. Finally the process invites women and men who often feel that they are in lonely and highly individualized professions to see themselves as colleagues who share a common calling. In doing so it acknowledges and honors the wisdom and experience we all bring to ministry.

Different cultures have varied assumptions about appropriate degrees of vulnerability, collegiality, and feedback. Although our model has been developed in a setting where Europocentric voices have predominated, it has been used with students from a range of cultural, racial, and ethnic backgrounds. In such a setting, cultural as well as personal differences emerge from and influence the process. For instance, some cultures are less willing to share negative feedback. Where possible we have tried to see that case reflection groups include at least two persons from any cultural group. In groups that expect to learn from their members, people seem to manage their differences. We invite you to learn as you go and let the authors know what you discover about how to make the approach more sensitive to persons of diverse cultures and to individuals in case study groups dominated by a culture other than their own. Theological case study has been most commonly used in seminary field education groups and in clinical pastoral education. We submit that cases are potentially useful for the members of any group committed to shared reflection on their practice of ministry.

BIBLICAL REFLECTION

Bible stories illustrate and inform this book, as they often do our reflection on cases. At times our reflection on a particular step in the case process called to mind a story from scripture. At other times—when we did not think we were working on the book—experiencing a Bible story would turn our thoughts to case work. Read in this way scripture connects us with the images, analogies, and stories that inform our tradition. In a process of "story matching," scripture points us to connections between our own questions and experience and that of God's people in other times and places. In this process the Bible both comforts and confronts us and our ministries.

We do not imagine that citing scripture "proves" our case. We hope our use of scripture in the book is illustrative of how we use it in case reflection and in life.

Scripture makes its claim on us as a location for dialogue with God's purposes. But we enter that dialogue expecting that different Christians, raising different questions out of different contexts, will come to different conclusions. Indeed, some of the richest reflection on scripture and case work has happened in groups which, respecting both scripture and their diversity, listen to differing interpretation of both the case and the Bible.

We also recognize that the reflection on biblical stories and images offered here is not a substitute for exegetical work with the texts. We gratefully acknowledge the way our reflection process has been enriched by colleagues from the biblical field, especially Peter T. Nash, who worked with us as a member of the field education staff. Our training and expertise is in other areas. But, as any responsible Christian must, we try to relate our questions and concerns to the faith of the Bible as we know and understand it. Clearly, the more fully a reflection group knows the cultural context and setting of the scriptures, and the more carefully they attend to the task of connecting their reflection on scripture and the contemporary challenges of ministry, the richer and fuller this process will be.

HOW TO USE THIS BOOK WITH A PEER GROUP

Whether in a formal class setting, or for informal group discussion, the book is designed to be used collaboratively. After working through all the case studies, you should have sufficient mastery of the method to continue working together without the book. As is true with any skill, continued practice will sharpen your ability to learn and grow together through case study.

Chapter 1 outlines the entire case process; chapters 2

through 6 lead the reader through the stages of preparing, presenting, and discussing the case; and chapter 7 discusses the implications of the process. Each chapter offers (1) a biblical image which connects the case process with the dynamic Christian tradition, (2) a sample case of supervision in, or reflection on ministry, and (3) a discussion of the issues around a particular part of the process.

Groups using the book are encouraged to begin writing and sharing their own cases very early on. Those just beginning to learn the case method might read the first two chapters for their first session, discussing the ideas presented during the first hour. Then, using the case discussion method outlined in chapter 1, spend the second hour reflecting on the case used as an example in chapter 2. For subsequent sessions participants are encouraged to read and discuss a chapter and its sample case in the first hour, and then in the second hour to work on a case prepared by one of the participants. In this way the abstraction of "ideal" cases is avoided; and, as a participant, you begin early in the learning experience to reflect on your own experience and that of your peers. At the end of five sessions, members of the group can decide whether they want to continue this process of mutual disciplined reflection on ministry.

The open sharing of our ministries encouraged here requires a commitment to confidentiality. In order for participants to be appropriately vulnerable, they must know that what they share about themselves, their joys and struggles in ministry, and about others in their ministry settings, will remain within the group. This covenant of confidentiality needs assent from every participant. The facilitator may appropriately remind the group, from time to time, that the open sharing by the presenter and participants is a gift to be treasured. Nothing said in the group is to be repeated outside the group. The presenter can affirm this commitment by disguising, as much as possible, the identity of persons in the case who might be known to participants in the group and by collecting the written copies of the case at the end of the session.

Chapter One

How Wisdom Is Shared Through Case Study

Someone in ministry, referred to here as "the presenter," offers in writing a critical incident, or story, from his or her own practice of ministry to a small group of peer participants for the purpose of consultation and theological reflection. The process of discernment and interpretation is directed by a designated facilitator. The goal is always to send the presenter back into ministry with greater self-understanding, further insight into the context of his or her ministry, and renewed confidence in God's presence and power.

Case study is a tool of ministry used in a branch of theological reflection that is loosely called practical theology. "Practical theology . . . is theological reflection and construction arising out of and giving guidance to a community of faith in the praxis of its mission."[1]

Case study invites engagement in a process through which assumptions about God, the world, others, and ourselves may be revealed. As we clarify and revise our assumptions, we are more likely to move toward fuller appreciation of God's presence and of the giftedness, woundedness, and courage in ourselves and one another. Because it helps us evalu-

---

1. James Fowler in Don Browning, ed., *Practical Theology* (New York: Harper and Row, 1983), p. 154.

ate the link between our beliefs and our actions, our words and our deeds, case study is a means of strengthening Christian discipleship.

The focus of such theological case study is an individual's practice of ministry. An understanding of the presenter's context of ministry will inform the reflection on his or her practice. In every case the goal is to strengthen the presenter's ability to analyze situations and to understand more fully himself or herself as a minister. We offer two analogies from scripture, which suggest a biblical framework for case study and set an individual's ministry within the activity of the people of God.

NATHAN AND DAVID

The story of Nathan confronting King David provides one biblical model for the work of critical reflection in ministry. In 1 Samuel 16 during the reign of King Saul, David enters the story of Israel as a shepherd boy who defeats the Philistine strong man Goliath. He dies on the throne of Israel at the beginning of 1 Kings. Meanwhile, in the book of 2 Samuel, we read of David's rule and his frequently meandering walk with God.

Frederick Buechner suggests that "just about every king seems to have had a prophet to be a thorn in his flesh and help keep him honest."[2]

Nathan's role was often to be such a thorn in the flesh for David. This description is a suitable analogy for the role of the peer group. When writing and discussing a case, the presenter is always revealing and concealing. Our process is designed to identify the questions, metaphors, and images, which get under

2. *Peculiar Treasures* (New York: Harper & Row, 1979), p. 114.

the skin and allow the presenter to bring forth the truth about herself and the ministry in which she is involved.

Analogies are of course limited. One danger in using the story of Nathan and David as an analogy for reflection in ministry is that it may encourage us to view the process in hierarchical terms, as though some were always prophets calling others to account. In fact, all are learners. Facilitators need the opportunity to learn by sharing their own cases, as well as to learn by facilitating the cases of others.

A second danger is that the prophetic analogy may lead us to view casework as though its only function were to expose our secret failings. In fact, case reflection has been prophetic in the authors' lives in that it has helped us to see more clearly our own gifts and graces and to identify our limitations. Through this process each of us has developed skills in reflection that help us to name the recurring themes and issues that we confront in our ministries and to minimize the price we, and those we serve, pay for our weaknesses. We want to introduce this process to readers in ways that affect not only their present learning but the practice of ministry throughout their lives.

Perhaps no incident in the long relationship of David and Nathan is more revealing than that involving Bathsheba and Uriah the Hittite. Of interest to us is the role and method of the prophet in naming what is going on.

> The Lord sent Nathan to David. He came to him, and said to him, "There were two men in a certain city, the one rich and the other poor. The rich man had very many flocks and herds; but the poor man had nothing but one little ewe lamb, which he had bought. He

brought it up, and it grew up with him and with his children; it used to eat of his meager fare, and drink from his cup, and lie in his bosom, and it was like a daughter to him. Now there came a traveler to the rich man, and he was loath to take one of his own flock or herd to prepare for the wayfarer who had come to him, but he took the poor man's lamb, and prepared that for the guest who had come to him." Then David's anger was greatly kindled against the man. He said to Nathan, "As the Lord lives, the man who has done this deserves to die; he shall restore the lamb fourfold, because he did this thing, and because he had no pity." Nathan said to David, "You are the man!" (2 Sam. 12:1-7a)

David's response to this vivid image is confession, followed by a change in attitude and action. The prophet suggests that God's plan for Israel is not dependent on the perfection of God's servant. But it is dependent on that servant's ability to see his actions in a new light and to return to his serving with new focus and purpose.

In presenting a case we invite others to take on the role of truth-tellers, helping us to see clearly our behavior and its implications. If ministerial case reflection is a theological process, then that truth-telling must relate our experience to our highest values, or—in Winquist's words—"to our vision of ultimate reality."[3]

Several elements of this story should help us reflect on ministry. Consider the need for the prophet and the prophet's focus. In his examination of the relationship between individual and societal ethics, Reinhold Niebuhr outlines the way that self-interest blinds us to the truth of our action. We need someone who stands apart from us to tell us the truth about our actions.[4]

---

3. Charles E. Winquist, *Practical Hermeneutics* (Chico, Calif.: Scholars Press, 1980), p. 25.

4. *Moral Man and Immoral Society* (New York: Scribner's Sons, 1932).

The role of the prophet is to tell the king the truth, to help the king see the meaning and consequence of his actions. In offering up our practice of ministry for reflection, we invite others to take on the prophetic, truth-telling role in relationship to us and our ministries. They point to the truth we conceal from ourselves about what we are doing and how others are affected by our actions.

Nathan zeros in on David and his responsibility for the situation. The subject of Nathan's reflection is not Bathsheba's role in what happened, or the appropriateness of the actions of her husband Uriah the Hittite, or even the soldiers who, on the king's orders, abandoned Uriah to his death on the battlefield. Nathan's focus is on the one who is present. We do well to remember that the presenter, in the same way David was, is the subject of the case presentation—not the others who appear in the case. The participants' role is to let the presenter see who he is in this situation and to understand more fully the implications of his actions. We conceal as well as reveal the issues in our lives and ministries. Like King David, it is because we are often blind to the meaning of our actions that the process is helpful.

THE "BENT-OVER WOMAN" AND THE "BENT-OVER MAN"

In another case of truth-telling, the story of the bent-over woman and bent-over man in Luke's Gospel (13:10-17) reminds those in ministry that they do not exist in a vacuum. They are only one party to the continuing conversation between God and people that forms, nurtures, and sustains communities of the faithful. Their actions affect the spiritual health of individuals and congregations.

Now he was teaching in one of the synagogues on the sabbath. And just then there appeared a woman with a spirit that had crippled her for eighteen years. She was bent over and was quite unable to stand up straight. When Jesus saw her, he called her over and said, "Woman, you are set free from your ailment." When he laid his hands on her, immediately she stood up straight and began praising God. But the leader of the synagogue, indignant because Jesus had cured on the sabbath, kept saying to the crowd, "There are six days on which work ought to be done; come on those days and be cured, and not on the sabbath day." But the Lord answered him and said, "You hypocrites! Does not each of you on the sabbath untie his ox or his donkey from the manger, and lead it away to give it water? And ought not this woman, a daughter of Abraham whom Satan bound for eighteen long years, be set free from this bondage on the sabbath day?" When he said this, all his opponents were put to shame; and the entire crowd was rejoicing at all the wonderful things that he was doing.

(Luke 13:10-17)

In this story, Jesus is the prophetic voice that calls the religious leader to accountability for words and deeds, and through the leader, calls the people to examine their understanding and practice of their tradition. Jesus shares God's power for healing and invites the claiming of this power. This story, which could be read as a case, is set in the context of a teaching conversation that Jesus is conducting in a local synagogue. In the course of his teaching, Jesus poses a problem to the community of believers. A woman appears who has been bent over for eighteen years by what the RSV translates as a "spirit of infirmity." The nature and the origin of her ailment are not mentioned. It is said only that she could not straighten herself.

24

Jesus notices the woman, calls out to her, and without requiring anything of her, announces: "Woman, you are freed from your infirmity." The ruler of the synagogue, bent over by legalism, complains. He turns from the moral claim, made by the presence of the wounded woman and Jesus' response, to make a counter claim. To the crowd he charges that the law against working on the sabbath has been violated by this act of healing.

Jesus will not allow himself to be shut out of the conversation. He turns and faces the synagogue leader, engaging him in theological reflection. Jesus points out that the people did work on the sabbath, contrary to their rhetoric. They fed and cared for their work animals, on which depended the people's economic survival. Jesus does not condemn them for this. He calls them to be truthful by pointing them to a wider circle of experience. Otherwise, they are in danger of overlooking God's work of healing and of confronting evil, the essence of sabbath and that which is central to their spiritual well-being, as they join God in this ministry.

The story is left open-ended. Here is a picture of God, with tender heart, asking the leaders and community tough questions through the deeds and words of Jesus. Will the community's interpretation and application of rules draw people into conversation with God or shut them out? This issue continues to have relevance for God's people. Will our reflections on our ministries shut people out or draw them into conversation with the Holy One? The faithful in all ages are invited to consider the meanings and implications the story has for their life together. How will they define and respond to the woundedness in their midst in the future?

25

In a surprising turn of events, the wounded woman and her healing becomes an image, through which others are invited to look for their own woundedness. Their hope resides in God's graciousness. In collaboration with God's purposes, distorted thinking and practices are healed. As in the case of Nathan and King David, the process of reflection can help leaders see their actions more clearly. The human tendency to displace responsibility onto others is confronted and challenged.

One of the lessons to be learned is that the designated leader of the community plays a crucial role in posing probing questions that direct the community's life and ministries. There is a parallel here with the role of the facilitator in the process of case study on ministry practice. The facilitator offers support and encouragement to the vulnerable case presenter. The facilitator encourages each participant to engage in critical theological reflection, to reflect on what is heard, what is said and what sense it makes, and to offer insights about the underlying assumptions and distortions made by the presenter. It is helpful to have someone frame the questions that let us see our actions in a new light, while remembering that the source of truth remains rooted in the gospel story of God's life with people.

The invitation of the case process is to bring our "stuff" before the Source of all wisdom. In that process all are equal. Because a case calls forth questions in all of us, whether facilitator, participants, or presenter, the process is one of mutuality. In the course of this dialogue, other options for thinking and acting are revealed. The case presenter is challenged to consider fresh options and is lifted up by signs of God's grace in her ministry and by new directions offered by peers. In turn, the presenter's ministry is a resource for peers in their practice.

SNEAKING UP ON THE TRUTH

Fresh understandings of ourselves and our ministries come when we find a different vantage point from which to look at our actions, or a new context in which to think about our experience. Sometimes we can hear the direct challenge of one who, like Jesus in response to the ruler of the synagogue, points out the inconsistency of our interpretations or actions. At other times we resist seeing ourselves in such descriptions.

The revealing and concealing nature of our self-reflection points to the reason for the form of Nathan's response to King David. It is hard, sometimes impossible, to hear the truth about ourselves and our ministries when it is spoken as directly as Jesus speaks in the parable of the bent-over woman. Often displacement is necessary if we are to see the truth. Nathan chooses a parable to allow David to sneak up on the truth about himself. Similarly, we have to find the metaphors, illustrations, and stories that allow the presenter enough distance to discover the truth and to connect with a tradition.

These are not the only biblical or theological analogies that may help us understand the process of reflection on our ministries. Nor do the authors deny the value of images and ideas from other sources. The reader can probably suggest others, such as those that rise out of educational, social, literary, or psychoanalytic theory. Whatever their source, these connectors both conceal and reveal certain things about the case. We live in a complex world in which metaphors from outside our faith tradition help us understand the tradition and our work in new ways. When Nathan declares, "You are the [one]!" his role is not unlike that of another commentator on the folly of kings who answered Lear's query, "Dost thou call me fool, boy?" with the rejoinder, "All other titles thou has given away. That thou was born with."[5]

But whether we are "synagogue teachers," "prophets," or "fools," the presenter is "king" and having heard the wisdom of others must finally decide whether or not it is truth to be heard and integrated.

THE PROCESS

We encourage a seven-step process much like that used for case reflection in a number of other seminaries and Clinical Pastoral Education programs:

1) Presenting the Case Aloud
2) Clarifying the Information
3) Sharing Personal Wisdom
4) Pooling Professional and Educational Wisdom
5) Claiming the Wisdom of the People of God
6) Reflecting on the Presenter's Ministry, and
7) Evaluating the Process

The steps are described briefly as follows. The group needs to covenant to spend a specific amount of time with the case, typically 60 to 90 minutes. The facilitator serves as timekeeper and leads the participants and presenter through the process, deciding how much time to give each step for a particular case.

---

5. Shakespeare, *Lear*, act 1, sc. 4.

1. Presenting the Case Aloud

Begin with a concise written description of an incident in ministry in which the presenter sets the background, describes the incident, and shares his or her analysis and theological reflection. (See the model for writing the case in appendix 1.) The presenter reads the case aloud so that we can hear the emphasis and interpretation he imposes. The participants note questions or insights that emerge as the presenter reads through the case.

Steps 1 (Writing), and 2 (Presenting and Clarifying) are discussed more fully in chapter 2.

2. Clarifying the Information

The next step is to clarify the information the presenter has offered. We are not yet offering analysis but seeking to understand the incident as the presenter represents it. Clarifying questions might focus on: the order of events, the relationships, the feelings and attitudes of those in the case, or the degree of emotional, imaginative, and intellectual intensity. Here it is important to clarify the issues the presenter wants us to focus on for consultation. The facilitator may want to close this section by asking the presenter if she wants to add any further clarification.

3. Sharing Personal Wisdom

At this stage the presenter is invited to be silent. At the end of the case reflection, the presenter will be asked what has been helpful in the process; in the interim his primary role is engaged listening.

In this step our goal is to connect the case and presenter to the lived experience of the participants and to become aware of what each brings to the case. The participants are asked what the case elicits in them. They may be identifying with the presenter—or someone else in the case. The events of the case may have called up powerful memories or emotions. These may help with or distract from the task of interpreting the presenter's case. In either instance it is well to acknowledge the connections we make.

See chapter 3 for a fuller discussion of this stage of the case process.

4. Pooling Professional and Educational Wisdom

We bring our professional and educational histories, as well as our personal wisdom and experience, to bear on the case. Here the goal is to focus that pooled wisdom so that it is accessible. Our own experience and training create a bias in favor of insights from social and psychological theory, issues of race, class, and gender, and the revelatory power of images from film and literature. In your reflection you will need to think about the sources of your own analytical gifts.

This process of pooling professional wisdom is described in chapter 4.

5. Claiming the Wisdom of the People of God

Questions of theology and spirit inform the entire case process. They shape the way we reflect on our own experience and our educational and professional wisdom. But here they are made explicit in order that the faith issues do not go unnoticed.

At every stage of the process the facilitator must make decisions of focus, guiding the group by the questions asked, and by the insights that are followed up on or passed over. Nowhere is this more clearly important than in choosing among the myriad religious approaches to the case. One can look for the way particular theological themes or concepts might add to our understanding of the case. Discovering biblical stories or images that illumine the case is helpful. Questions that grow out of the faith tradition of the presenter or participants might help the group identify and name God's action within the case. The facilitator's own gifts, the specifics of the incident reported, and the experience of the presenter and participants will determine the questions to be asked.

See chapter 5 for a fuller consideration of this stage of the case process.

6. Reflecting on the Presenter's Ministry

Having struggled to bring together our lived experience, the insights of our professional and educational backgrounds, and the wisdom of God's people, we are now brought back to a clearer focus on the "king," who has observed the conversation of the gathered fools and prophets. What can we say about the presenter's ministry as it is embodied in the actions of the past and the possibilities of the future?

In light of the pooling of wisdom about what happened in the case, and what it means to us, the group's attention turns to reflection on the performance of the presenter. What has she done well? What further work is needed with persons in the case or in the presenter's self-understanding?

The last steps in the case process, "reflecting on the presenter's ministry" and "evaluating the process," are explored in chapter 6.

31

7. Evaluating the Process

Finally, as we recall whose ministry is at the center of our reflection, the presenter is invited back into the conversation and asked: What has been most helpful in this process? What insights have you gleaned?

32

Chapter Two

Writing, Presenting, Clarifying

When members of a group gather to hear and to process a case, their session usually begins with oral, informal checking-in with one another about current concerns in life and ministry. There may also be a time of prayer or the offering of a "religious resource"[1] that sets the tone and serves to gather members of the group. However, when the ministerial case is presented, it is essential that the presenter write it so all may read as well as listen. The written case provides the participants a text, which is more reliable than their memories of what the presenter said, and requires the presenter to commit to a concise account and particular—focused—reflections. The written case is, of course, a story—an interpretation of the events described. However much we attempt to tell the truth about ourselves we are inevitably involved in both "hiding" and "revealing."

The writer-presenter chooses to share a particular issue or incident out of a desire for consultation on her ministry. Through opening the situation to consulta-

---

1. A term first used by James Ashbrook, our Garrett-Evangelical colleague, in the context of field education groups, to include the presenting of some resource (e.g., a symbol, image, poem, object, prayer, reading) that influences a person's life at depth and that may evoke responses from other participants in a group or class. This may be devotional in character. But the primary goal is not to serve the worship needs of the other participants but to share the faith life of the presenter of the religious resource.

tion, the presenter hopes to come to some fresh awareness and deeper understanding. Thus, at some point in
the written case, it is important that the presenter indicate on what elements she wants the most assistance.
The connecting biblical image, to which we will return
later in the chapter, is an adaptation of Jesus' question
to Bartimaeus, "What do you want [us] to do for you?"
(Mark 10:51).

As outlined more fully in appendix 1, it is recommended that each of the following sections be included
in the writing: (1) background and context; (2)
description of the event; (3) analysis of important issues
and relationships; (4) evaluation of the presenter's own
effectiveness; (5) theological reflection.

WRITING

The written case should be brief, limited to two sin-
gle-spaced pages. Part of the discipline of case writing
includes condensing the most crucial information,
analysis, and reflection into what is essential for understanding and critical for learning. Writing succinctly
facilitates reflection and discussion by others. Writing
the case also clarifies the presenter's understanding of
the event, in such a way that he can more readily reflect
on it toward further growth. Writing the case at once
calls back the experience and creates a degree of analytical distance.

Clearly expressing an event objectifies the situation,
enabling useful reflection on it and potential learning
from it. We relate the incident in the form of a story. By
this we do not mean that the case is fictional, or that
the presenter should feel free to take liberties with the
characters or plot. Instead, like any good narrative, a
case incident tends to have a beginning, middle, and

end. The need to interpret the incident involves the presenter in an inevitable ordering of the case.

The presenter should write the case in a way that reminds the participants of the importance of confidentiality. For example, by changing names or using initials or titles, the need to protect persons can be underscored. Yet even when this is done participants may recognize the persons described in the case. Therefore, at the time of presentation and discussion, it is essential to reaffirm the principle of confidentiality. For this reason we also urge the return of all case sheets to the presenter at the conclusion of the discussion.

PRESENTING

Having written the case following the five-point outline just described, the presenter normally makes enough copies to enable the members of the reflection group to follow along as the presenter reads the case. Reading aloud is an important part of the process, since oral nuances give additional data or emphases to the presenter's relationship with the event or persons involved. Participants may note questions or insights in the margins as the reading proceeds.

Some facilitators work at making the connections between the case and the participants' lives and ministries even during the reading. The facilitator might halt the presenter periodically to ask participants for connections in their lives, biblical and literary analogies, or other questions that help to connect them to the case. Most facilitators have usually held these questions until step three, "Sharing Personal Wisdom."

The facilitator may wish to ask particular participants to be alert to specific elements in the case, such as: nonverbal communication, a sense of direction or move-

35

ment, conflict, avoidance or resistance, intimacy or aloofness, self-awareness of the presenter, the insights emerging from a particular analytical method or question, or particular pastoral roles.

CLARIFYING

After the reading, the facilitator invites participants to ask the presenter questions for clarification. Here the goal is not analysis, interpretation, reflection, or evaluation, but a fuller understanding of the case as the presenter has represented it. If the group begins to analyze the case prematurely, the facilitator gently brings them back to the clarifying purpose. The following kinds of questions might be directed by the facilitator to the participants:

- What is unclear?
- Do you need further help from the presenter in understanding the relationships and events of the case?
- Is further clarification needed concerning the feelings and attitudes of the subjects in the case?
- Has the presenter been clear about the kind of consultative help he or she wants from us?

When members of the group sense that their questions have been answered, the facilitator may give the presenter opportunity to offer any further clarification he or she feels is needed. Then the presenter is invited to keep silence and listen carefully as the group discusses and reflects on the case.

A CONNECTIVE BIBLICAL IMAGE

The connecting image evoked by the clarifying questions of the colleagues is that of the man born blind,

36

son of Timaeus (Bar-timaeus), who is asked by Jesus, "What do you want me to do for you?"

> They came to Jericho. As he and his disciples and a large crowd were leaving Jericho, Bartimaeus son of Timaeus, a blind beggar, was sitting by the roadside. When he heard that it was Jesus of Nazareth, he began to shout out and say, "Jesus, Son of David, have mercy on me!" Many sternly ordered him to be quiet, but he cried out even more loudly, "Son of David, have mercy on me!" Jesus stood still and said, "Call him here." And they called the blind man, saying to him, "Take heart; get up, he is calling you." So throwing off his cloak, he sprang up and came to Jesus. Then Jesus said to him, "What do you want me to do for you?" The blind man said to him, "My teacher, let me see again." Jesus said to him, "Go; your faith has made you well." Immediately he regained his sight and followed him on the way.
>
> (Mark 10:46-52)

The Synoptic Gospels present Jesus as one who neither forced himself on people nor insisted that they follow in his way. Rather Jesus invited, evoked, taught by story the way of God among humans. Jesus took seriously the freedom and inner authority of each person. In the accounts of the healings, Jesus most often offered choices to and asked questions of the persons who came to him with their concerns, their problems, their illnesses. With Bartimaeus, Jesus asked directly: "What do you want me to do for you?"

That is a key question for all case groups. Participants first listen clearly for what kind of assistance and consultation the presenter most needs and wants. It is important that the presenter somewhere identify the area or areas of the case on which he wants consultation and help. The presenter is the authority in the choosing and writing and presenting of a case. He is inviting consultation on a very specific issue, which may have evoked a recurring theme in the presenter's life and ministry. But if the presenter has not stated this need clearly, or if a multitude of questions have been raised in such a way that there is no possibility of addressing all of them, then the clarification stage provides a block of time for the presenter to respond to the group's question, "What do you want (us) to do for you?"

What follows is a case a ministerial supervisor shared with other supervisors in the hope that they would help him reflect on his ministry of supervision. The case describes a supervisory session between the male supervisor and a female seminary student working with him. Following the written case are pertinent portions of the clarification stage of the discussion, which took place within the supervisor's peer group to whom this case was presented.

WILLIAM'S CASE: "A CONFLICT OF BACKGROUNDS"

1 *Background*
2 This is a case study of a supervisory session I held
3 with a female seminarian who was working as a
4 chaplain intern in a retirement home. I am a
5 past-middle-age male minister who serves as
6 chaplain at the home. The home serves two con-
7 stituencies. First is a group, largely female, who
8 will need some financial help to stay in the home
9 through their life expectancy. The second con-
10 stituency is a group, largely upper-class, of peo-
11 ple who are required to have considerable assets
12 to be admitted to the home. As one of her learn-
13 ing goals the chaplain intern indicated a desire
14 to learn to minister to people of a different

15 social class than she had known. I, as the chap-
16 lain, interpreted this to mean that she would like
17 to have some experience with economically privi-
18 leged people in the setting the home afforded.
19 At this supervisory session I raised the question
20 about whether or not she felt comfortable with
21 the more privileged people with whom she had
22 come in contact.

23 *Description*
24 The chaplain intern was nonplussed when I
25 asked that question. It was obvious that I had not
26 understood her learning goal. My understanding
27 was that she wanted to become comfortable with
28 people who came from an environment she had
29 not experienced. What became evident to me
30 was that the intern felt that privileged people
31 needed to be reminded of their privilege and
32 responsibilities in no uncertain terms. She told
33 me that she felt the preaching in the chapel
34 catered to people who had money, that they were
35 seldom reminded of their responsibility as Chris-
36 tians, and that she found it very difficult to relate
37 to people who seemed to be so indifferent to the
38 needs of others. I countered by saying that I had
39 no responsibility for who was admitted to the
40 home, that I tried to treat all of the residents the
41 same, and that I felt she was being too judgmen-
42 tal about the responsibility that people must
43 bear. It was obvious that here was a woman who
44 had already made up her mind about many of
45 the people in the community, and who was com-
46 mitted to telling them how far short they had
47 fallen from living faithful lives. For my part, as
48 chaplain, I saw the intern as a person of limited

49 experience who was putting herself in the role of
50 judge and jury, making judgments about people
51 whom she hardly knew.

52 *Analysis*
53 The chaplain and the chaplain intern, though
54 not that much different in age, were vastly differ-
55 ent in life experience. She came from a farm
56 community where she had rarely met movers and
57 shakers, where she mistrusted those who were
58 privileged, and where she automatically assumed
59 that they were all indifferent to the plight of
60 those who had less than they had. On the other
61 hand, I had served thirty years of a thirty-eight-
62 year ministry in parishes where people were
63 largely privileged. I had understood that needy
64 people were not necessarily poor people, and
65 that ministry need not mean "throwing gravel in
66 peoples' faces every Sunday." What was going on
67 here was the classic dilemma of how to minister
68 to the "haves" with a gospel which seems to favor
69 the "have-nots."

70 *Evaluation*
71 I felt I, as chaplain, was basically ineffective in
72 this supervisory session because I became defen-
73 sive about thirty years of ministry spent with peo-
74 ple who were the "haves" of society. The supervi-
75 sory session called into question in my mind my
76 own faithfulness to the gospel. I was challenged
77 by this novice, as I had been before by those who
78 had not borne the full responsibility of ministry.
79 I also lost patience with one who seemed not to
80 want to understand. The intern on her part, I

81 believe, saw me as one who had sold out to easy
82 answers and a soft life.

83 *Theological Reflection*
84 This supervisory session raised a number of
85 interesting questions. How much does a supervi-
86 sor have to justify himself or herself to a semi-
87 narian? Does a supervisor have to feel that he or
88 she is seen as a model of ministry at all times
89 and in all places? What kind of differences of
90 opinion emerge when life experience is vastly
91 different? It is assumed that the supervisor has
92 considerable experience and that a seminarian
93 has little. Is this really true? In any exchange
94 between two persons, no matter what their expe-
95 rience, there is the possibility of God's hand.
96 Does God raise the issue here of judgment and
97 acceptance? In Christian ministry there is always
98 the issue of the prophetic and the pastoral. How
99 can the prophetic be truly prophetic without
100 cost? How can the pastoral be truly pastoral
101 without cost?

CLARIFYING DISCUSSION FOR "A CONFLICT OF BACKGROUNDS"

Facilitator: William, thank you for describing the supervisory setting and the internal and external conflict you
experienced. Are there questions for clarification from
others to William, so that we understand the case well
enough to reflect on it when he goes into his silent
time?

Stanley: Yeah, I have one. It sounds like the intern was
being judgmental of the people at the home, and that
you were then being judgmental of her. What kind of

41

trust level had been built between you two? I was wondering, for instance, how far into the school year this event occurred.

Presenter: This session occurred about the end of the first month of her being at the home, so some trust had begun, but not a great deal as yet.

Nancy: It sounds from the case like you really laid it on the intern about her judgmentalism. How did she respond to your reaction to her?

Presenter: She was taken aback, and expressed annoyance and the feeling that I just "didn't get it."

Nancy: Did you continue the conversation at that point, or was that it?

Presenter: Yes, we continued for a time, yet we had reached a kind of impasse. I wasn't sure at that point whether we would ever resolve it or whether we could take it farther. That's why it is an important case for me to bring here.

Bess: You say in the case that you saw the intern as "a person of limited experience." Was she really that limited? After all, you indicate that she and you were not that different in age. Was she really limited in experience or did she simply have a different kind of experience from yours?

Presenter: She certainly had a different kind of experience from mine, and, yes, I felt she was limited in her experience with the type of people we have at the home.

Tom: You've raised some really important questions for all of us in your "theological reflection" section. But I'm not sure which ones are most important for you at this point. What do you most want to work on with us? How can we help you in your supervisory work with this intern?

Presenter: I guess I am most concerned about how to be accepting of this intern (and others who have experience different from mine) while continuing to value the integrity of my experience. I would like to see her with greater clarity and objectivity. And I think I need help on recognizing more clearly what God's direction is in all of this.

Facilitator: Are there any further questions for clarification for William, before we invite him to listen to us reflect on the case? [Silence and head shaking] William, are there any other matters you want to clarify with us that haven't been dealt with in the questions?

Presenter: No, I think I've stated everything that is needed at this point.

Facilitator: O.K. Then, I invite you, William, to listen quietly now as we reflect on our own feelings about the case.

CONCLUSION

Since our purpose in presenting William's case is to illustrate the writing and clarifying stages of the case process, we will leave the discussion at this point. In agreeing to let the case be used here, William commented that just stopping to put the case on paper had been a useful discipline, which had begun a process of clarifying his strong emotional response to this student and incident.

"A Conflict of Backgrounds" is a tightly written, well-stated presentation. William evaluates himself honestly and clearly, seeking to be fair to the intern's perspective, while not undervaluing his own ministry. He raises important questions, and he responds honestly to the questions for clarification asked by other supervisors in the peer case-study group.

In "A Conflict of Backgrounds," the case group is not being asked to pass judgment on an intern who did not understand the problems of upper-class residents. Nor are they being asked to resolve the conflict between the chaplain and the intern. They are asked to be attentive, to hear with new ears and see with new eyes a conflicted supervisory situation between a supervisor and an intern whose life experiences are widely disparate.

As they begin Stanley asks about how early in the school year William's supervisory conversation with the student took place. This helps to clarify the circumstances. He presses to understand not only where it comes in the chronology of the year, but the level of trust that had been established. By her query, Nancy seeks to understand the emotional tone both William and the student manifested at the time. Bess questions what William means by asserting the student's "limited" experience. All of these questions help the group to see the interchange more fully. In response William is able to articulate clearly both his sense of the student's position and emotional investment and his own sense of "impasse."

44

William has raised several important questions concerning the supervisory role, experiential differences, judgment and acceptance, prophetic and pastoral functions. The supervisory group members rightly ask that he name more precisely the key areas on which he wants their consultation. Such clarification aids the case process, so that the group members do not run all over the map with their pet issues, but are focused on the presenter's concerns. They are guided by Jesus' question to Bartimaeus—"What do you want (us) to do for you?"—as they listen to the presenter's response to the same.

Following this time of clarifying, William's peers are able to identify and empathize with what William, in the evaluation section of the case, called his defensiveness. By letting the peer group be a place where William's needs can be acknowledged, and his career in ministry affirmed, they help him to reclaim his focus as supervisor. The student will continue to be a challenge for William, and to raise anxiety in him about her ability to work effectively with the residents of the home where they minister. But William returns to the supervisory relationship with greater self-awareness and commitment to working on the student's formation for ministry. In your own work with case reflection, you, as a participant, will want to give particular attention to this clarifying stage of the case process.

By remembering to clarify, you can stay focused on the writer's presentation of the case while it is being read. Resist the temptation to interpret the case until you have listened and read carefully. At this point simply mark words or phrases that seem significant, passages that are unclear, or places where you need a character, role, or relationship identified.

After the reading, look back over your copy of the case. What do you need the presenter to clarify in order for you to understand the case and its context? Our purpose at this stage is not interpretation or argument. Rather, taking as little time as possible, be sure that you understand the facts of the case, the key players, and the presenter's concern in bringing the case.

When the most pressing questions have been asked, the facilitator invites the presenter to be silent. When you are a presenter, you have the opportunity to be an active listener rather than a part of the dialogue. Thus you can avoid the trap of defensiveness and premature debate of your colleagues' interpretations and insights. Plan to make notes of the comments that you want to remember. At the end of the process, you will be asked what has been most helpful, and if you feel misunderstood you will have opportunity to clarify.

Ministerial case reflection begins with the presenter's assertion of what consultation is wanted. But, as we will see in subsequent chapters, the reflection process may lead the participants to make other connections and raise questions the presenter has not considered. Often these will offer you, as presenter, new ways of considering your experience; you are urged in presenting to remain open to hearing the questions the case gives rise to for others.

Jesus addressed Bartimaeus directly, but the account is preserved so that others may consider the implications of Jesus' question. The case process can help any participant to grow, and valuable reflection can be generated even if it so happens that the presenter's issues are not directly addressed. But the presenter is the designated learner—the Bartimaeus of the moment—and, precisely as we ask at the beginning what it is that the presenter wants from the group, we will ask again at the end what responses to her or his questions have been heard, and what else has been helpful.

Chapter Three

Chapter Three

Personal Wisdom

After clarifying questions have been asked and answered, as described in the last chapter, the case group turns to a time of sharing personal wisdom. For a brief time the focus shifts from the presenter to an opportunity for the participants to identify feelings and images in their own experiences which are evoked by the case just presented. When have they known similar people or been in situations that called forth similar feelings, issues, or ideas? What images do they recall? Here the participants seek to enter personally into the environment of the case. In the next stage the participants will try to gain access to their knowledge, but here they offer up their experience.

The questions raised grow out of the assumption that the case reflection is not simply for the presenter but a part of the continuing self-reflection of each participant. The presenter offers his or her ministry in hope of coming to new insight and to enable reflection on our calling. This process of connecting with the experience of the participants is a step toward deepening that mutual reflection which enriches the learning of all who participate. Each of us has an ideology and a personal history. To share personal wisdom opens us in a revealing way to others. We begin to be more honest about how our own lives and commitments focus our engagement with and questions of another's case.

Perhaps nowhere in the case process is the analogy between case and story more apt than at the stage of personal wisdom. We respond to the case as we do to a literary work, noting how it connects with our passions and acknowledging what it calls forth in us.

The presenter is invited simply to listen in silent attentiveness. Often this proves to be a time of connecting during which the presenter comes to see that an experience that may have left him or her questioning judgment, gifts, or even calling itself, has been shared by others. At other times it will be obvious that the case has called up powerful memories for a participant, which need to be heard in order to make sense of the participant's later reflection on the case. It can be especially helpful for the participants to respond with this level of vulnerability.

Another connector from biblical tradition presents itself in the parable of the sower flinging seed to the earth and discovering later that the seed has fallen in diverse places—some falls where it will be taken by birds, others where it is too rocky or thorny for growth, and yet others where the soil is good and receptive.

> That same day Jesus went out of the house and sat beside the sea. Such great crowds gathered around him that he got into a boat and sat there, while the whole crowd stood on the beach. And he told them many things in parables, saying: "Listen! A sower went out to sow. And as he sowed, some seeds fell on the path, and the birds came and ate them up. Other seeds fell on rocky ground, where they did not have much soil, and they sprang up quickly, since they had no depth of soil. But when the sun rose, they were

scorched; and since they had no root, they withered away. Other seeds fell among thorns, and the thorns grew up and choked them. Other seeds fell on good soil and brought forth grain, some a hundred-fold, some sixty, some thirty. Let anyone with ears listen!"

(Matt. 13:1-9)

One pastor who has often supervised others uses this parable as an image for ministry. She says that she was never attracted to the parable, because she heard it interpreted as though we were dirt—some of us good dirt and some of us bad dirt—in which God was scattering seeds. "It's not much fun," she comments, "to be dirt—even if you turn out to be good dirt." But in reflecting on her ministry with a Chicago congregation she exclaimed, "We're not dirt, we are the sower!" And she helped the congregation to think about their efforts to be in ministry as a kind of sowing—all of it called forth by the Spirit's exuberance.

We find the image of the sower a helpful way to think about the case process. In fact, it may be instructive to think about ourselves both as sowers and as soil. Like the planting Jesus describes, there is a certain messy excess to it. The presenter scatters the case among the participants not knowing whether it will fall on empty ears or be heard with shallowness, or whether it may touch depths and evoke promising ministry experiences. This first stage in the reflection process lets the participants pay attention to their own "earthiness." Where is the case calling forth something in them, and where do their pasts make them shallow, rocky, or thorny?

In turn the participants are themselves scatterers of seed. They offer up their personal experiences, their professional wisdom, their theological reflection, and their consideration of the presenter's ministry, not knowing what of this will take root in the presenter or in another participant.

Jerry's case, "First Funeral," is used to illustrate this stage of the process. It arises within the ministry of a seminary intern facing his first funeral. He is honest about his feelings of fear, anxiety, and awkwardness. He asks for help in trusting more in God's grace to move and minister through him. The colleagues consulted here include other students involved in full-time internships and a seminary field education staff-person who had many years of experience in congregational ministry.

Following the case are excerpts from the personal wisdom section of the group's reflections, in which they share what the case evoked experientially in each of them.

JERRY'S CASE: "FIRST FUNERAL"

1   *Background*

2   Two months into my intern year my supervis-
3   ing pastor was going out of town for four days,
4   which required me to cover for her. Tuesday
5   evening I received a call from the local funeral
6   home asking that I conduct a funeral service on
7   Thursday for "Mr. Jones." I had hoped I would
8   have observed or assisted in a funeral with my
9   supervisor before doing one myself, but circum-
10   stances did not turn out that way. "Mr. Jones" was
11   a ninety-year-old man who died in his daughter's
12   home. I did not know him or the family. Only
13   one daughter was a regular attender of my super-
14   visor's church.

15 My supervisor was not leaving until Thursday
16 morning, so I was able to get some guidance
17 from her regarding what she normally does for a
18 funeral service. We were able to visit two of the
19 Jones daughters in their homes, so that I could
20 be introduced and my supervisor could express
21 her condolences. I planned to attend the viewing
22 that evening to try to get acquainted with other
23 members of the family.

24 *Description*

25 I went to the viewing alone. Upon entering, I
26 sat down because I did not see any of the
27 daughters or the funeral director. I felt very
28 awkward and uncomfortable, for I did not know
29 what to do. I felt as though I should know,
30 because I was the pastor conducting the
31 funeral. I was supposed to help lead the people
32 who had lost their loved one, yet I did not know
33 what to do.

34 I got up again to try to find the funeral direc-
35 tor to "check in." After speaking with her, I
36 found the daughters I had met, and a few other
37 family members. I was at a loss to know what to
38 say. Not knowing how long I should be there
39 made it all the more difficult. Yet I think I kept a
40 calm facade.

41 I nervously tried to put together the service
42 and homily that evening and the next morning. I
43 decided not to greet the Jones family before the
44 service so that I could collect my thoughts. The
45 service seemed to go smoothly, though afterward
46 I found out it is customary to shake hands and
47 offer formal condolences before departing from
48 where the service is held.

49   I rode in the lead car to the grave site and led
50   the brief committal service. I felt uncomfortable
51   again after I had finished the service, while the
52   family members stood around.

53 *Analysis*

54   This funeral service took me by surprise.
55   Jumping in, as I was forced to do, caused me
56   quite a bit of anxiety, yet it provided me with a
57   real "hands on" learning opportunity. The view-
58   ing was most difficult because I was least pre-
59   pared for it and I had only met the family that
60   day.

61   I feel much more comfortable in circum-
62   stances where I have a clear task or purpose and
63   when I know what to expect. The unsettling
64   part of the first funeral was that I expected peo-
65   ple to look to me to lead them and I did not
66   feel adequately prepared or knowledgeable to
67   do so. I need help in exploring more what it
68   means to be in the role of pastor in these cir-
69   cumstances.

70 *Evaluation*

71   After looking back on these events, I believe
72   I was in ministry helping the bereaved individu-
73   als, though I may not have felt it at the time. At
74   the reception after the funeral, some of the
75   family members who had heard that this was
76   my first funeral commented that I had done
77   very well. I suppose that I did minister, though
78   my anxiety clouded my vision of my doing min-
79   istry.

80 *Theological Reflection*

81   I am beginning to see that ministry is a balance of
82   preparation and allowing God to work through us.
83   This situation was an anxiety-producing series of
84   events because I was not always able to find that bal-
85   ance. Discovering the balance between our prepara-
86   tion and the work God does is key to ministering in
87   a healthy way.

88   I see two themes here: faith, and God's grace
89   that is often evident despite my lack of faith. I am
90   aware that my faith in God's power to minister
91   through me could stand some growth. God's
92   grace demonstrated in how others respond to
93   our ministry is more readily available than I am
94   willing to accept. Perhaps reflecting further on
95   the story of Moses when he was called to minister
96   will help deepen my insight into faith.

PERSONAL WISDOM EVOKED BY "FIRST FUNERAL"

After Jerry finished reading the case and responding
to clarifying questions, the facilitator invited him to
remain silent and hear how the other participants connected with, and reflected on, his case. Knowing that
the participants would be making conscious and uncon-
scious connections with their own lives and ministries,
the facilitator used the "personal wisdom" time to help
the participants call forth those connections.

Facilitator: As we hear Jerry's story, why don't we share
from our own personal experience what this evokes in
us.

Dave: Early on in my intern site, I got a call from my
supervisor. "I know it's your day off, but can you come

down to the hospital emergency room? We need your help." So I changed clothes and went down. A boy had been in an accident and the parents were there. Two boys were involved; one of them was being transferred to a bigger hospital. So my site supervisor was going to go with him. They were not church people; he just got called in. So he said to me, "You stay here with this family." I didn't know what to say. I kept saying to myself, "It doesn't matter what you say; just being here is enough." Finally the parents and I got to go in and see their son. He was pretty banged up and just kept repeating things. I eventually had prayer with them and when everything seemed to have stabilized, I left. But I had that feeling of not being adequate, of not knowing what to say and the anxiety of saying the wrong thing.

Facilitator: Was there something that went flitting through your mind that would happen if you didn't find the right thing to say?

Dave: Well, I try to avoid saying things like, "It's going to be O.K." I was afraid there might be either false hopes or things that are not really comforting. I was afraid that in trying to be consoling, I might say something I didn't realize.

Jennifer: That's part of it. I remember recently somebody came up and said, "Thank you for going to the funeral." And I said, "My pleasure." [Laughter] When somebody is close to me it really isn't a big deal. But some things just come out of your mouth. When Jason [of the seminary staff] was at my churches I did my first baptism. He was trying to help me sort out how much of my anxiety was because he was there observing, and how much was because it was my first baptism. I don't like "firsts."

Maybe I'm moving into theological reflection, but the most powerful, comforting thing for me is faith and grace. The faith is in God.

Facilitator: Imagining you're not alone and you have a partner in this undertaking.

Jennifer: At times I don't even imagine that. I don't think the word "partnership," but "right now" the Holy Spirit is going before to prepare a place for my ministry. And also that it's not under your own resources that you will be able to minister and do what you need to do. There are many times, when I wonder, "What do I say?" I have no idea. Or "How do I do this?" I have no idea. But somehow by the presence of the Spirit everything moves along the way it's supposed to move.

Facilitator: It seems as though we're addressing how we've arrived at guidelines for trusting ourselves or God or other people. We've been drawing on resources of our tradition: prayers, scripture, mentors along the way who have shared with us that wisdom from our religious tradition. Anything else to say about times when you've been in this kind of situation? And what resources you've found yourself drawing on?

Paul: I remember that, when I was in CPE, and had to do a funeral for someone I didn't know, part of my anxiety was that I didn't know much about the deceased. So it was hard to know what comfort to offer the mourners. I didn't know if the person who died had lived an active life of faith, whether he died with a sense of calm and completeness, confident that he continued in God's presence. That would have been a comfort for all of us. If the family are not peo-

57

ple of faith, or if I simply don't know whether they are, part of my anxiety about what I'm going to say is anxiety about what comfort or assurance they can hear.

Beverly: In my first parish, the first person to die was not a member of the church, though his wife was. He was a former Catholic, a Korean War veteran, in his thirties, and had committed suicide. They were parents of three young kids. Suddenly the call came, and I was a very young, naive pastor in my mid-twenties. I went over to the home, wondering, "What in the world will I say to help?" I had never before faced suicide. It was that same sense as others have described—what now? I sort of prayed my way over there. The widow just talked and talked. She seemed to need a listening presence and somebody she could weep with and lay it all out to and share the problems of depression he had as a veteran. It all evolved, so that I was released from my anxiety, in the course of being a listening presence. But I certainly didn't know what was going to happen between the phone call and the drive over to her house.

Jennifer: Having a pastoral presence and knowing that our presence doesn't have to be something that we have to say or something that we have to do. But just sitting there and being there.

Facilitator: You really are moving us into what we know from our education or professional practice . . .

CONCLUSION

The case evokes many memories and stories of group participants' early pastoral experiences. There are memories of anxiety and vulnerability, arising from the unknown and from fear of failing or "doing the wrong thing." Jerry's case offers his peers the opportunity for such sharing of personal feelings, thoughts, "wisdom"— in terms of experiences of vulnerability as well as discoveries of grace and affirmation.

The participants identify strongly with the presenter. Dave, closest to Jerry in age and experience, immediately names a similar situation in which he was called, not to the funeral home, but to the hospital emergency room. Like Jerry he was cut off from the consultative support of his supervisor and was unsure what would be helpful. Both of them remember that it seemed to them they were effective ministerial presences—but the more powerful memory is their anxiety about their purpose and competence.

Jennifer lightens the moment with a joke in which she did respond inappropriately at a funeral. She uses the funny story of saying "my pleasure" to the one who thanked her to express her own connection with Jerry's case and to suggest that it would not necessarily have been the end of the world if Jerry had said the wrong thing. This allows Jennifer to express her evangelical confidence that the Holy Spirit is at work within our ministries—even when we feel less than confident.

Paul shares his own experiences of funeral anxiety within a CPE setting. Beverly, the faculty member, remembers a similar incident from her own early ministry. It is clear that Jerry's experience is not unique. Jerry is widely liked and his gifts for ministry are appreciated by both his peers and supervisors. Part of his struggle has been to recognize his gifts and trust his strengths. By their empathy the group helps him to trust that his anxiety in a new situation is not the evidence of some lack of ministerial gift or calling. He is helped to hear the analysis which follows this time of sharing personal wisdom.

This was for Jerry a confirming and comforting beginning. The openness established at this stage allowed the participants to dig deep as they reflected on Christian understandings of death, the social and religious function of the funeral, and the pastor's experience of role anxiety in the face of these realities.

At other times one or more participants may have an experiential connection with someone who appears in the case other than the presenter. For instance, in reflecting on William's case, in chapter 2, one of the other supervisors shared her emotional connection with the intern who works under William's supervision. Although this may not be as immediately affirming for William, such moments are also valuable connectors with the case, serving to clarify the participants' insights, deepen the group's reflection, and thus help the presenter see himself or herself more clearly.

Throughout, the facilitator may be thought of as a sort of redactor. The facilitator must help the group sense the moments when what is shared offers a helpful connection between the participant's experience and the case and the moments when it moves away from the issues raised by the presenter. The facilitator must also judge when to bring this time of sharing personal connections to a close so that the group may focus on the presenter and the presenter's case. It is the facilitator who takes this ranging, sometimes contradictory, conversation and tries to impose some degree of order on it. Some of what is flung out will have fallen on barren soil, but some of it will bear fruit "thirty-fold, sixty-fold, and a hundred-fold."

Chapter Four

Professional Wisdom

Having acknowledged our personal connections to a given case, which may sharpen or cloud our vision, we now bring our professional wisdom to bear on the case. But what do we mean by "professional wisdom"?

We think of everything a participant knows by virtue of education and experience to be a part of the professional wisdom he or she brings to the case reflection. This includes, but is not limited to, what we know about religion or the practice of ministry directly. For instance, one of the authors, with an avocational interest in narrative theology and film, often examines a case as though it were a plot, or turns to popular film for analogies that help the group to understand and interpret the case. Another, with a greater understanding of family systems and group theory, draws on those resources.

The distinction between "personal" and "professional" wisdom may seem arbitrary. It becomes clearer if one remembers that the primary objective in sharing personal wisdom is self-revelation, giving expression to personal memories of parallel or analogous incidents or narratives in the participants' own experience of ministry. The primary goal of professional wisdom is the analyzing of the case for the benefit of the presenter and the group.

In facilitating, it is tempting to suggest that the facilitator's questions are primary and should always be asked. But the proper agenda for a facilitator is to unlock what the participants have to offer. The facilitator can remind the group of their wisdom with questions appropriate to their background. Sometimes these will be tossed out to the group as a whole, while at other times the facilitator may want to call on the unique experiences of a particular participant. For instance, a participant with counseling skills might be asked to set a psychological framework, a literature major might be asked to provide a connection to modern fiction, and a sociologically adept participant asked about the social context of the case. As members of the group come to know one another, the facilitator will be able more easily to elicit responses from within the participants' areas of expertise.

In your case reflection, you may want to look at the assumptions about human nature in the case and in your varied responses to the case. Or you might consider how your knowledge of the social structures of race, class, gender, and power can help the presenter and peer reflection group understand the case. Or, as with the case discussion used as an example in this chapter, cross-cultural reflection may give the presenter a wider range of experience within which to consider the meaning of her own ministry.

The challenge is to see as clearly as possible what is going on in the case. This calls for insight into the motivations and interests of the presenter, the other persons in the case, and the community or institutions providing the ministry setting.

Participating in a group committed to disciplined reflection on ministries provides the opportunity to hear the diverse perspectives brought from the participants' varied backgrounds. Here we consciously attempt to call forth that diversity, listening for the perspective that can allow the presenter to see her ministry in a fresh light.

When we offer our understandings as a gift to honor the presenter's ministry, we recall the anointing of Jesus in the twenty-sixth chapter of Matthew's Gospel:

Now while Jesus was at Bethany in the house of Simon the leper, a woman came to him with an alabaster jar of very costly ointment, and she poured it on his head as he sat at the table. But when the disciples saw it, they were angry and said, "Why this waste? For this ointment could have been sold for a large sum, and the money given to the poor." But Jesus, aware of this, said to them, "Why do you trouble the woman? She has performed a good service for me. For you always have the poor with you, but you will not always have me. By pouring this ointment on my body she has prepared me for burial. Truly I tell you, wherever this good news is proclaimed in the whole world, what she has done will be told in remembrance of her." (Matt. 26:6-13)

One of the striking things about the story is that this unnamed woman does not ask the host, Simon, if she can offer her gift, nor does she ask Jesus if he wants to be anointed. Something about her experience of his ministry calls forth the extravagant gift of expensive ointment. At a time of repose in the midst of Jesus' ministry a gift and blessing are offered. Recognizing a precious gift within Jesus, the woman offers up something precious of her own.

As participants we pour out what we have of value as a gift to one who, like Jesus at Simon's house, is in a time of rest and reflection in the midst of ministry in progress. We offer what we know, what the case calls forth from us. Because of the diversity of our gifts, we cannot predict what the case will evoke. We cannot be certain whether our insights will be helpful to the presenter. Like the disciples, the other participants may not think our offering appropriate; they may be tempted to criticize, even reject it. But, like the woman at the house of Simon the leper, we offer up what the case calls forth from us.

Jesus comments that the precious ointment prepares his body for burial. That is, the offering is a gift which helps him be ready for what lies ahead. Similarly, our gifts of professional wisdom are future-oriented. When we analyze the context and interactions that shaped the case incident, we hope these will help the presenter return to her ministry with new understandings of what is going on.

At the end of the case process, and perhaps at subsequent gatherings if the group continues to meet, the one who presented the case can name and bless the offerings that have been most helpful in reframing her ministry.

Consider what happens when Kim, a Korean woman, presents a case out of her experience working in a Euro-American congregation. Kim is disturbed by an incident in an ecumenical women's Bible study where she has responsibility for educational leadership. She chooses to share it with a group of three older seminary colleagues: Jessie (an African American woman), and two Anglo women, Judy (a middle-aged divinity student) and Carrie (an experienced pastor who has returned to the seminary to work on a Ph.D.). An Anglo clergywoman and seminary instructor serves as facilitator.

The presenter introduces her case with the suggestion that, in hindsight, she realizes she was dealing with cultural differences in approaches to gift giving.

KIM'S CASE: "THE TWENTY-DOLLAR THANKSGIVING"

1 *Background*
2   I am leading a midweek, midday Bible study
3 group. Usually six or seven people participate.
4 Most of them are older women. About half of
5 them are members of the church I am serving.
6 The rest of them go to different churches. It was
7 one month after we started that one of those who
8 belong to other churches carefully asked me
9 whether they could give me financial compensa-
10 tion. I explained that I was compensated by the
11 church and that I did not want any other type of
12 financial gift.

13 *Description*
14   One week before Thanksgiving, after the class
15 was over, a person from another church gave me
16 a card saying, "This is from all of us." I opened it.
17 It was a Thanksgiving card. A twenty-dollar bill
18 was included. I expressed my surprise and
19 embarrassment. They said they wanted to thank
20 me, and the money was just a partial expression
21 of their hearts.

22 *Analysis*
23   It seems common that people in ministry
24 receive compensation and gifts other than the
25 regular salary, when involved in special ser-
26 vices. In this particular case, I feel that those
27 from other churches somehow thought our
28 relationship was not mutual. They wanted to
29 compensate in some way for the service they
30 are given.

65

31 *Evaluation*

32   I received the money, although I did not want
33 to. I thanked them, because I wanted to. What I
34 really wanted to do was to return the money on
35 the spot, but I thought that might hurt their
36 feelings. I dropped the money in the offering
37 plate of my church. I think I want to have an
38 area to support with money I receive from any
39 pastoral service. Then, I should announce pub-
40 licly to the people I serve that any gift will be
41 given to that specific area.

42 *Theological Reflection*

43   I find the theme of *service* in this event. "Ser-
44 vice based on no expectation of reward" is my
45 ideal—no reward, neither spiritual nor finan-
46 cial. I want always to be prepared to face aban-
47 donment and despair when I serve as a pastor.
48 Yet ideals can be both blissful and disastrous.
49 The meaning of pastoral service seems to me
50 something that we are shaping and reshaping
51 rather than something that is given us.

PROFESSIONAL WISDOM EVOKED BY "THE TWENTY-DOLLAR THANKSGIVING"

Kim's concern, that she respond faithfully to the gift
from her Bible study group, is one close to the hearts of
her peers. They are quick to share the stories of their
own experience. After they do so, with the facilitator's
assistance, they make the transition to draw on their
professional wisdom in analyzing Kim's case:

Facilitator: What do we need to consider from our professional knowledge as we think about whether some-

66

one in ministry should accept a gift from her parishioners?

Judy: In a class in ethics and society we have been talking about social relationships, of what it means to stand in solidarity with the poor. Does accepting financial gifts encourage people in such a culture to misunderstand the nature of servant ministry?

Jessie: We might consider Kim's special status. She is a student who is not yet in full-time ministry, and the members of the group probably understand that. To them she may represent a financially poor person whom they can stand with. I think they would be glad for her to use the money to meet her personal needs.

Judy: Yes, but Kim has shared with us her commitment to solidarity with the poor—those who are abandoned or in despair; she needs to consider what obligation comes with the gift. People must not think they need to give her gifts to receive her ministry, or that those with more to give will receive more of her love and care.

Facilitator: I remember accepting a loan from a parishioner once to buy badly needed car tires, only to discover that she expected all my attention as her personal chaplain in return. That was one of the most painful but powerful learning events in my own ministry. I've been more sensitive as a professional to reflecting on the meaning of exchange of gifts since then.

Judy: We have been talking about how Kim's understanding of social relationships informs her understanding of ministry. But her sense of human nature is also at work. Frankly, I think she expects too much of herself. It is good to want to be able to identify with those who are feeling abandoned and in despair, but it is unrealistic to expect to serve without any reward. When I worked with the Girl Scouts, we found that if someone kept giving out without receiving some kind of reward, either material, spiritual, or psychological, that person would run out of steam in nurturing others. Perhaps Kim needs to learn to graciously accept the appreciation of the people she has touched.

Facilitator: Our discussion has considered human nature and the nature of ministry as they are expressed in accepting or refusing a gift. Let me ask you a functional question. Does what the gift is used for make a difference? Is it preferable if she uses the money to enable further ministry? Are these ethical concerns answered if, as Kim suggests in her case, she tells the group about a ministry she will use the money to support? or if she used the money to buy a gift for the group as a token of appreciation?

Carrie: I've used gifts to buy a resource I've needed in ministry such as a Bible commentary. That might be particularly appropriate with a gift from the Bible study group.

Judy: Remember that different traditions have different understandings of how those in ministry are to be compensated, and whether such gifts are appropriate. For example, don't Roman Catholics have a tradition of giving gifts to priests and the church for special services rendered, such as masses for the deceased? From their point of view, perhaps, a gift to Kim would have been natural. A gift for her religious leadership—a compliment for her abilities and care. How would this be understood in a different denominational or cultural setting?

Jessie: Gift giving and receiving mean many different things to those involved. As an African American, I want to be able to give back by passing on my tradition. Two friends did this recently by coming to hear and support me in my preaching. They traveled a distance to do this, and then they even insisted on buying my dinner. I resisted and then realized all I had to do was to say, "Thanks."

I don't know if it comes through family or culture or the way the Bible is understood, but in the black church people like to give back something for what they have received of value. It is a symbol of appreciation and an expression of power. A claim that those who receive also have something to give. I think we have to look at motivation and the spirit in which something is given.

Carrie: In Euro-American culture, we have tended to value things by putting a price tag on them. Kim wants to communicate that what is valuable doesn't have a money tag on it. At other times Kim has expressed her concern that in Korea people are increasingly affected by capitalistic values of placing a materialistic price tag on everything. Some ministers of larger churches receive great material gifts. This contrasts with the smaller "people's churches" of the *minjung,* where everyone shares the limited goods. For Kim, part of the issue is how to keep her witness clear.

Jessie: As a younger person in her own culture, Kim would be expected to honor the elderly. Here, the elderly were honoring her. That must have made it hard for her to receive their gift. Perhaps these cultural values are part of her discomfort.

Judy: Maybe, if we share that vision of the *minjung,* both Kim and I need to think about when we should receive—at least modest gifts. Another cultural factor is that this incident takes place around a very "American" holiday, Thanksgiving. I don't know if there is a similar holiday in Korea. But within the U.S. culture of most of the women in Kim's Bible study group, this would be a time of year when such gift giving would be particularly appropriate. What one sees on the surface at Thanksgiving is a day of family celebration and excess. But it is also a time when churches and other groups in the community remember to give to others—particularly to the poor. I think it is also a time to express gratitude to those for whose gifts we have been thankful through the year. Those may be the cultural circumstances in which the gift is offered.

Carrie: When I was younger and new in ministry, parishioners seemed to regard me like a daughter or granddaughter. My feelings were always mixed. I perceived that small tokens were given to encourage me and so they could take pride in my accomplishments as they would in their own children. I was glad for the affection and affirmation; at the same time, I wanted to be thought of not as a child but as an adult professional. Psychologically it was a confusing experience, as I expect it is for Kim.

Facilitator: Gifts from others can provide a way to serve, but a reflective pastor needs to consider when, if ever, it is appropriate to receive a gift, when a gift can be used to meet personal needs and when it should be used for ministry. Perhaps, to choose wisely, Kim has to understand what she wants to communicate by her actions and the psychological effect on her and others of accepting or rejecting the gift.

Carrie: Absolutely . . . but it's not just a question of Kim's own understanding. We need to think about the giver's understanding of the gift's purpose and, perhaps, the nature of our social contract or covenant with the congregation we serve. There is also the issue of the wider cultural understandings of the gift and the obligations that come with it.

Facilitator: We have been offering Kim our different individual and cultural interpretations of what happens in groups, of how respect and appreciation are rightly expressed, what solidarity with the poor means, and our cultural understandings of what a gift means and what obligation comes with a gift. Let's bring this sharing of professional wisdom to a close and see if our theological reflection can inform, and be informed by, what we have said thus far.

CONCLUSION

Each of the women, as participants in the case group, has offered the gift of her own professional wisdom and expertise. They offer themselves and their histories, cultures, and professional experience—even as the woman with the alabaster jar of costly ointment did centuries ago at the house of Simon the leper. Members of the case group reflect on the ethics of accepting gifts from those they serve, while seeking to understand ministry in terms of mutuality and while not falling into the trap of favoritism. Judy speaks of the value of receiving as

71

well as giving. She refers to the meaning of gifts in other religious traditions. Both the facilitator and Carrie offer learnings from their parish ministry experience. Helpful questions have been raised about the function of monetary gifts. Jessie speaks of the importance, in her African American heritage, of supporting one another in quite tangible ways. Carrie also reflects on the "giver's understanding of the gift's purpose."

The group moves on to discuss, in the theological reflection section, what it means to be a gracious recipient of a gift and of how that might also be an act of solidarity with others. They are intrigued by the question of when a cultural tradition is to be accepted as a given, and when, out of higher loyalty, Christians need to confront and stand over against the values of the culture in which they serve. They also spend more time reflecting on the implications of being set apart for professional ministry, and on the special obligations that might come from a ministerial position.

Through offering their gifts of professional wisdom, the group participants respond further to the overarching question in the case process, What is going on here, in this situation? They give the presenter the gift of other perspectives from which to view the incident. Similarly and far more dramatically, the woman with the alabaster ointment offers Jesus, and those with whom he was meeting at Simon's house, another perspective. The gift she poured out was "costly," which led to her actions being sharply questioned by Jesus' disciples, who saw it as a waste of money. Jesus sees it differently and says so. Jesus sees the woman's surprising and lavish gift as moving him and his community toward the future; "she has prepared me for burial" (Matt. 26:12b).

The group assists Kim in looking toward her future in regard to monetary gifts from parishioners. In her closing reflection on the case, Kim reported that she found the discussion stimulating. She indicated that she felt supported, both as a woman in ministry among other women in ministry, and as a Korean woman among women from other cultures. She further indicated she was not sure whether she would be more open about accepting a gift in the future, but told the group she hoped to be able to discuss her embarrassment and its sources with the women in her study group. Her peer participants expressed their heightened understanding of the issues involved and thus were aided in their present and future ministries.

Chapter Five

Theological Reflection

Reflection on a ministry case presentation is concerned with theology and spirit throughout the process. Having brought a range of experience to bear upon the case, we now turn to the language, images, and categories unique to our faith tradition. Here we purposely consider what light the history of Israel, the stories of Jesus, the tradition of the church, and our own experiences of the living God shed on the case. We seek to articulate categories of theological reflection that can focus our discernment and inform our lives of faith.

If we understand ministry to be more than just another of the helping professions, if we understand it to be a part of the response of God's people to God's activity in history, then this discernment is a crucial part of our consultation on one another's ministries. This is particularly the case in a secular culture, where the vocabulary and images of faith are no longer the common language of either art or moral discourse.

Learning a religious vocabulary reminds us of who we are and of the communities to whom we are accountable. By claiming the theological categories of those communities, we set our issues of ministry in the context of the continuing struggle of God's people to be faithful.

Later in this chapter, members of the peer group raise a biblical image that is helpful in thinking about the call to theological reflection. They invite us to consider our role as participants in a case study, which is similar to that of the disciples in the story of feeding the 5,000.

> Now when Jesus heard this, he withdrew from there in a boat to a deserted place by himself. But when the crowds heard it, they followed him on foot from the towns. When he went ashore, he saw a great crowd; and he had compassion for them and cured their sick. When it was evening, the disciples came to him and said, "This is a deserted place, and the hour is now late; send the crowds away so that they may go into the villages and buy food for themselves." Jesus said to them, "They need not go away; you give them something to eat." They replied, "We have nothing here but five loaves and two fish." And he said, "Bring them here to me." Then he ordered the crowds to sit down on the grass. Taking the five loaves and the two fish, he looked up to heaven, and blessed and broke the loaves, and gave them to the disciples, and the disciples gave them to the crowds. And all ate and were filled; and they took up what was left over of the broken pieces, twelve baskets full. And those who ate were about five thousand men, besides women and children. (Matt. 14:13-21)

When evening comes the disciples want Jesus to send the crowd away to buy something to eat in the villages. Jesus replies, "You give them something to eat" (Matt. 14:16*b*). In the next verse the disciples, not trusting the adequacy of what they have to offer, reply, "We have nothing here but five loaves and two fish." But Jesus takes what they have and blesses it. When the crowd has been filled the disciples collect twelve baskets of left-overs.

When we agree to share in the reflection on the ministry of one of our peers, Jesus makes a similar demand on us. "You give them something to eat." Like the earlier feeding of God's people in the wilderness, where manna was provided (Exodus 16), there is a particular food that God and God's people have to offer. At this stage of the process, having brought to bear the full insights of our wider training, we focus the discussion to ask what the language and categories of theological discourse, liturgical dialogue, and biblical narrative suggest about the case.

A parallel between ministry case studies and biblical narratives may be pertinent here. The gospel writers attempted to discern the mind of Christ as stories were told of Jesus' interacting with individuals and groups in their religious communities and wider social settings. In the act of putting these interactions in story form, the gospel writers posed theological questions and revealed competing moral claims. Out of these questions and conflicts, communities of God's people discern and reformulate calls to minister.

Over time the formal discipline of writing and discussing cases builds confidence and ability in theological reflection. With practice members of the group become comfortable in calling forth the religious images and concepts that speak to them. The facilitator evokes their insights by posing theologically probing and provocative questions.

It has been our experience that for many groups this is typically the hardest part of the case reflection process. This can be true for pastors, for Christian educators, for theology students, and for persons without formal theological education. But over time and with encouragement, the gift for theological reflection within a case group proves to be more than adequate. Often the theological insights overflow like the baskets of leftovers among the 5,000.

At this point in the case process, there is the danger that participants will simply bracket the earlier discussion and move on to unrelated and disembodied theological reflection. One way to prevent such bracketing is to pause, before the transition to the overtly theological reflection, to ask the group to summarize or highlight the key insights that they have had thus far. This can help participants carry earlier material forward so that it informs, and is informed by, their theological reflection. To draw again on our biblical story, the faith teaching moment in the feeding of the 5,000 must not lose its connection with the earlier recognition of the people's physical hunger.

The goal of the theological reflection stage of the case process is interactive dialogue between the case material and our relationship with God. Images and questions of faith are both informed by and further illuminate the earlier expression of participants' experience and wisdom from other fields. They may also be challenged or confirmed by the case itself.

As with the discussion throughout, the facilitator decides how to focus the conversation. Considering the expressed needs of the presenter, the material of the case, and the background and interests of the group, the facilitator raises questions that open the doors for theological reflection.

The facilitator might begin the process by asking what theological questions are raised by the case itself. Does the case challenge the professed beliefs or theological perspectives of the participants in any way? If so, how? If not, how are participants' theological perspectives confirmed or clarified by the case? After such discussion, the facilitator might then ask what biblical stories, images, or themes are evoked by the case. Are there biblical persons, narratives, parables, events, or images of God that illuminate or are analogous to the case at hand? Within the participants' memories of biblical passages, which ones find their way to the forefront of consciousness in relation to this particular case?

The facilitator may also raise the question of whether there are moments in the history of the church that the case calls forth. What images or understandings of the church are operative in or challenged by this case presentation? What assumptions about church process, structure, authority, hierarchy, and ecclesiology are at work?

Alternatively, the facilitator might think about questions that call on the unique doctrinal or historical focus of a particular tradition. Those in the Anglican and Methodist traditions might use the Wesleyan quadrilateral to look at the incident in light of that which is (1) revealed in scripture, (2) illumined by tradition, (3) brought alive in personal experience, and (4) informed by reason. Lutheran piety might begin by looking for the relationship between law and gospel in the incident. Presbyterians, remembering the tension between God's will and the public will and order, might ask how the "Lord of the conscience" guides in this matter. Evangelicals and Pentecostals might remind us to look for where the Holy Spirit is active in the lives and incidents revealed.

Appendix 2 offers a further range of opening questions that can help to open or focus the theological discussion. You may want to turn to those in preparing to facilitate or participate in this stage of the process.

Now we consider a case prepared by a full-time intern and a portion of the theological reflection her peers and facilitator raise as they work with her case.

VICKIE'S CASE: "APPROPRIATE AUTHORITY"

1 *Background*
2   Soon after my arrival, my supervising pastor
3   expressed concern and frustration about having
4   to set up and begin a confirmation class. He told
5   me that it was always hard to find a suitable time.
6   Kids come from school activities without having
7   had supper, are tired, and have trouble settling
8   down to accomplish anything.
9   I was aware of a new confirmation curriculum
10   that was supposed to be excellent. The confir-
11   mand is paired with a model "saint" of the con-
12   gregation, and they work together one-on-one.
13   The pastor's role is facilitative. The pairs decide
14   how long they want to work together. It is very
15   much an experiential approach. My supervising
16   pastor looked the materials over, presented them
17   with my help to various committees he deemed
18   necessary, and the decision was made to give this
19   approach a try.

20 *Description*
21   It was up to my supervisor to get the ball
22   rolling. Initially, he tried to do this, but some-
23   where he lost control of it, and people's doubts
24   began to creep in. Adults began to become intim-
25   idated about working in pairs. The momentum

80

26 was lost. Though I was the "youth pastor," it had
27 been decided that it was not up to me to head
28 this project. Territories had been clearly marked,
29 and this was not my "turf." My supervisor did not
30 discuss it much with me, except for saying that
31 he needed to take care of some things. People
32 were waiting for him to follow through.

33   To deal with the resistance to the process that
34 was developing, it was decided that a meeting
35 would be held with confirmands, their parents,
36 potential mentors, the pastoral staff, and any
37 administrative council members who wanted to
38 be present.

39   The youth came with their own proposal for
40 confirmation. They wanted to stay as the cohe-
41 sive group that they had become. They wanted
42 to have their class meet together on Sunday
43 morning, using their present Sunday school
44 teacher as their instructor, with parental back-
45 up. Outside activities related to confirmation
46 would be limited because of the many other
47 claims on their time.

48   Some of the adults at the meeting proposed
49 various approaches differing from the mentoring
50 approach. Fears were not eased about the new
51 approach.

52 *Analysis*

53   What eventually surfaced were the contrasting
54 expectations of those at the meeting, their strug-
55 gles, their fears, and concern about who was in
56 charge. The youth kept bringing up the fact that
57 they were only fourteen and fifteen years old.
58 The parents said it was important to them that
59 their kids be confirmed before graduation from

81

60 high school. The pastor did not express strong
61 opinions one way or the other. Many were asking
62 the questions: What does confirmation mean—to
63 the church? to the confirmands as individuals?
64 What does it require to be confirmed? What is
65 the appropriate process and the appropriate con-
66 tent for confirmation education? No one seemed
67 to respond adequately to such questions.

68 *Evaluation*

69 I was invited to sit in on the meeting. I raised
70 questions and responded to questions. I listened
71 and tried to speak only when I really felt strongly
72 about an issue. My goal was to help surface fears
73 and questions. Looking back, I don't think peo-
74 ple who came were open to hearing the opin-
75 ions of others. And I found it difficult to help
76 people be more open to listening and to coming
77 to some common agreement. I think I func-
78 tioned effectively in terms of surfacing fears and
79 questions. But I sense I need some help in iden-
80 tifying the lines of authority and in discerning
81 how to help people come to a mutually agreed-
82 upon decision. Responsibility for what is wanted
83 and needed must be taken. Requirements must
84 be set. The problem is that people in this
85 church seemed unable to do this, and I was
86 unable to assist them to move in that direction.

87 *Theological Reflection*

88 What is a Christian group, experientially and
89 as based in scripture? If the church had had a
90 strong youth group, would the meeting have
91 gone differently? Would participants have
92 understood experiences of faith and how these

93   are nurtured? We send out unspoken signals as
94   we seek to negotiate standards for behaving as
95   the church. We need to be alert to what we are
96   teaching by what we are doing.

97   What occurs to me scripturally are stories from
98   John 5 about the paralytic and from Mark 10
99   about Bartimaeus. In these stories, Jesus raises
100   the questions, "Do you want to be made well?"
101   and "What do you want me to do for you?"

102   Everyone involved in this case is faced with
103   making decisions. Faith is a required dimension
104   of these decisions. Making a commitment is nec-
105   essary.

THEOLOGICAL REFLECTION EVOKED BY "APPROPRIATE AUTHORITY"

Not surprisingly, in a group that included other interns, the questions of the supervisor's follow-through and the church's openness to new ideas introduced by the seminarian elicited immediate connection during the personal wisdom stage of the discussion. The group moved on to reflect on the nature of small-town churches, group dynamics, strategies for change, and the nature of personal and role authority.

The peer group was somewhat critical of the supervisor's lack of decisive leadership and wondered whether he was genuinely committed to this new program. They affirmed Vickie in her clarity about the limits of her authority and were intrigued by her questions about the nature of the church and the meaning of confirmation. They also addressed her request for consultative assistance on how to help persons in the church community come to some decision when there are strong differences of opinion.

The group of interns and their facilitator represent a spectrum of ages and a variety of church settings. They vigorously describe various images of the church, the values and difficulties of Christian community, and the meaning of confirmation.

Facilitator: Let's turn our attention to making explicit the theological implications of this case. Does this case challenge your theological assumptions? What biblical and theological images of God and of the church do you see in our discussion thus far? Earlier Vickie named some questions asked by Jesus: "Do you want to be made well?" and "What do you want from me?" Do other questions or biblical images come to mind?

Joan: There is the question about confirmation. What does it mean in an individual sense? Is it a rite of passage into adulthood? We connect it with church membership. Is there scriptural support for confirmation? For the timing of it? How does a person really come to belong to the church?

Frank: What is the meaning of belonging in the Christian community? What does it mean to be a part of the body of Christ? In those churches that baptize infants, parents take vows for their children, and they are welcomed into the congregation. Later, these children make their own vows at confirmation. This sounds like stages of belonging, into which members of the body of Christ help incorporate other, younger Christians.

Bea: Confirmation is more than an individual matter.

Dwayne: One of the images that come to my mind is faith as a communal process, a matter for the whole

84

fellowship of the church. But the people Vickie has described seem unready to mentor others into the church.

Joan: They took vows when they were baptized or confirmed. If they had understood what they were doing, they wouldn't be confused about their role now, I think.

Dwayne: I think this is a problem in lots of churches.

John: I am reminded of the story of the feeding of the 5,000 and the disciples who said, "Jesus, there are all these hungry people and there's nobody to feed them. Send them away." And Jesus said, "No, you give them something to eat." There are all kinds of people being told or needing to be told in this case, "You give them something to eat." Those folks who have been identified by their sisters and brothers in the church as persons of faith, capable of being mentors, are among them. People we look up to in our churches need to hear from their peers and pastors, "You give them something to eat. We have confidence that you can do this."

Frank: I think the pastor in this case needs to figure out what it means for him to give leaders and kids something to eat. I think Vickie is struggling to understand who it is that she is supposed "to feed." Who knows what she has to offer and how she might offer it?

Facilitator: Remember in 1 Corinthians and in Ephesians the sections about calling forth gifts from the people of God? Gifts differ and they need to be called forth. I would say in this case that the pastor's primary responsibility is to call forth the gifts of mentors who call forth the gifts of children and youth. In this church, the call-

85

ing process may have broken down. Gifts are being denied because decisions have not been made clearly and decisively.

Jack: It makes me think about the crucifixion. After Jesus' death, those left behind were floundering. They weren't sure where to turn.

Dwayne: I support Vickie's not rushing in to fix things, as though she were the Messiah. She could have easily fallen into that trap.

Facilitator: We are starting to move into the next section of our process, the evaluation of and reflection on the presenter's ministry.

CONCLUSION

Prior to the theological reflection, the group has considered the issues of power dynamics and group process, which made it difficult for the intern and supervisor to work effectively together. This led to great confusion as church members tried to choose a direction for their confirmation program. When the overtly theological questions are called forth, members of the group begin to reflect on the meaning of confirmation—for the church as a community of faith and for the individuals involved in the decision. They remind one another that this conflict of authority and process is about how and why young people enter the church. They consider implications for the faith life of the congregation.

The group discussion of confirmation may have been a distraction from the core issue of staff relationships and conflicting patterns of authority. The facilitator might have been more active in focusing the discussion on the theological challenges arising from the underlying conflict between intern and pastor and from the tendencies of the laity to abdicate responsibility for fear that they would fail or lack expertise. Many questions are raised by participants. Some might have been helpfully pursued in greater depth.

Biblical images bring members of the group back with a new focus on the question of what it will mean for Vickie and others to be in ministry in this situation. As they go on to consider how Vickie has been effective in her ministry, and how she might return to it with fresh direction, they are in a position to relate their reflections on the implications of membership in the church to their earlier concerns about power dynamics and group process. This allows them to engage the theological issue of power in the church and the possibility that power might be appropriately shared by clergy and laity in mutual ministry. In the course of this dialogue, other options for action are revealed to presenter and participants alike.

The central metaphor of the feeding of the 5,000, chosen to describe this section of the process, is suggested by a participant in the discussion. John recalls that Jesus charged the disciples, "You give them something to eat." To their amazement, in collaboration with Jesus' power, the disciples were able to provide more than enough of the basic food and nurture needed to maintain life. The feeding of the 5,000 is a transformative event for all involved.

The invitation to you, the reader, as you reflect with your peers, is the same. When one of the participants in your case group holds up her ministry for your reflection, you are being asked to respond in ways that maintain and encourage the life of that ministry. The feeding and nurturing of a ministry, through the recollection and articulation of pertinent biblical images, events in church history, and continuing experiences of the presence of God, are central elements in the transforming of an incident where the presenter previously felt "stuck" or blocked. Giving "something to eat" in the form of theological reflection is a potentially nourishing gift to all participants.

What you are invited to do in theological case reflection is similar to what is happening today in the base communities of Central and Latin America, of inner-city Chicago, and other places throughout the world.[1]

Through the base communities' three-step method of reflection—observe, judge, act—many northern Christians have learned how to more clearly bring the message of the gospel into conversation with the stuff of people's lives.

In theological case reflection, covenant groups, and in the base Christian communities, people's lives inform their Bible study, even as their study of the Bible informs and illuminates their work and worship. Just as Jesus urged the disciples to give the people something to eat, so also we encourage one another. When we make sense of the gospel and, through common study and sharing, are nourished by the Scriptures, we will find connections to our lives and the work to which we are called. The accounts of the ministries of participants in base Christian communities testify to that truth.

Questions arise from the cases you and your peers present: Who is God, what does Christ ask of us, what is the nature of the church, and what is the shape of the

---

1. For example, see Ernesto Cardenal, *The Gospel of Solentiname* (Maryknoll, N.Y.: Orbis Books, 1982); and George Cairns, ed., "Base Christian Communities" issue, *The Chicago Theological Seminary Register* vol. 81, no. 1 (Winter 1991).

created order within which we act? Through mutual theological reflection, the case presenter and all participants are challenged to rethink certain familiar stances, to be undergirded by signs of God's grace in their continuing ministries, and to be empowered to move in fresh directions in their lives.

Chapter Six

Reflection on the Presenter's Ministry

I n light of the pooling of personal, professional, and theological wisdom, the group now reflects directly on the ministry of the presenter in the case at hand.

Three concerns shape our reflections here:

First, in what sort of ministry has the presenter been engaged? Is it a priestly, prophetic, or pastoral ministry? Is it a teaching, spiritual companioning, or mentoring form of ministry?

Second, where was the presenter particularly effective? What worked well? What didn't work well? What could have been done differently to facilitate the situation more fully?

Third, what implications are here for ministry in the future? What are some next steps that the presenter might take in ministry with these persons in the presented situation? What learnings and growth might there be for the presenter as he continues in ministry?

This stage of the process offers opportunity for members of the group to evaluate the presenter's ministry and to envision themselves in his place. Supportive counsel for the reflection is a strong element of this stage. Yet it is less an advice-giving, problem-solving time than it is an evoking of gifts, of skills, and of potentially fresh learnings for all present. Peer consultation is especially evident at this point in the process. Here, participants consider how they may continue to be supportive of the presenter in his or her ministry, including a commitment to pray for and with the presenter.

Finally, after a considerable period of silent listening on the part of the presenter, he is invited to come back into the verbal dialogue. The presenter is asked: What has been most helpful to you in this consultation? What learnings have you gleaned?

The connecting image from the biblical tradition for this part of the case process is that of midwife. Consider the story of the midwives of Israel:

Now a new king arose over Egypt, who did not know Joseph. He said to his people, "Look, the Israelite people are more numerous and more powerful than we. Come, let us deal shrewdly with them, or they will increase and, in the event of war, join our enemies and fight against us and escape from the land." Therefore they set taskmasters over them to oppress them with forced labor. They built supply cities, Pithom and Rameses, for Pharaoh. But the more they were oppressed, the more they multiplied and spread, so that the Egyptians came to dread the Israelites. The Egyptians became ruthless in imposing tasks on the Israelites, and made their lives bitter with hard service in mortar and brick and in every kind of field labor. They were ruthless in all the tasks that they imposed on them. The king of Egypt said to the Hebrew midwives, one of whom was named Shiphrah and the other Puah, "When you act as midwives to the Hebrew women, and see them on the birthstool, if it is a boy, kill him; but if it is a girl, she shall live." But the midwives feared God; they did not do as the king of Egypt commanded them, but they let the boys live. So the king of Egypt summoned the midwives and said to them, "Why have you done this, and allowed the boys to live?" The midwives said to Pharaoh, "Because the Hebrew women are not like the Egyptian women; for they are vigorous and give birth before the midwife comes to them." So God dealt well with the midwives; and the people multiplied and became very strong. And because the midwives feared God, [God] gave them families. Then Pharaoh commanded all his people, "Every boy that is born to the Hebrews you shall throw into the Nile, but you shall let every girl live." (Exod. 1:8-22)

Members of the peer group reflecting on the presenter's ministry engage in a midwifing responsibility. They coach, encourage, support, assist the presenter in the process of learning, naming, and "birthing." In the Exodus narrative, the pharaoh of Egypt begins to fear the enslaved Hebrews for their strength and the number of their offspring. He decides to have all male babies killed at birth, and seeks to enlist the aid of midwives. Shiphrah and Puah, the Hebrew midwives, refuse to obey the pharaoh's orders, since they "feared God." Then, to protect themselves from Pharaoh's wrath, they tell Pharaoh that the Hebrew mothers are so strong that the babies are born before the midwives arrive.

The point of this connecting image is that the participants in the case group are there as encouraging colleagues for the presenter. They are there not to destroy what is being birthed in the presenter, but to help bring to life that which is growing and developing in her. This understanding balances the image of prophet in chapter 1. There wisdom seems to flow from the participants to the presenter. Here the participants serve by aiding what is growing in and emerging from the presenter.

As you read the case, "The Wrath of Mom," and follow the process of the reflections on David's ministry by the group and by David himself, watch for how the function of the midwife is present. The presenter of this case is a male seminarian, in the midst of a full-time intern year, in a town parish, working primarily, though not solely, with youth. The seminarian is young, serious, conscientious, friendly—a responsible person who is committed to his ministry. He deals here with a parishioner who challenges him in an area of his feelings where he is not very practiced—that of anger and blame.

DAVID'S CASE: "THE WRATH OF MOM"

1 *Background*
2   Two weeks before Christmas the junior high
3 youth group had a Christmas party. They wanted
4 to pick "secret Santas," spending no more than
5 $5. Those who were there for the decision picked
6 their secret partner. Later I began calling others
7 who had not come to the meeting to get a count
8 of heads. Because I wasn't sure about exactly who
9 was attending when I talked to certain people, I
10 told them to buy for "a boy" or "a girl." Thus
11 some kids had particular people in mind, and
12 some only a particular gender. At the party then
13 I had to see that all the kids went home with pres-
14 ents. I went around and asked each person if the
15 present was bought (1) with a specific person in
16 mind, or (2) with a specific sex if not person, or
17 (3) for either sex, and (4) would it be O.K. to
18 give the present to someone other than the
19 intended person? I brought an extra present to
20 help out. Everybody went home with a present.

21 *Description*
22   As I was cleaning up after the last person left at
23 11:30 P.M., the phone rang. It was Dorothy, the

94

24 mother of one of the boys who had been at the
25 party. She was livid with me for switching pres-
26 ents around. She claimed they had bought base-
27 ball cards for a specific person because he col-
28 lected them. She was very angry and offensive
29 and on the attack. I decided to be a "non-anxious
30 presence," so I didn't try to defend myself. I told
31 her I had asked each person individually whether
32 that person's present could go to someone else
33 or not. "Well, that's not the way it came across to
34 my boys." Then she made a personal affront:
35 "I've seen you talk to thirteen-year-olds, and you
36 have a lot to learn!" After she seemed to be
37 through, I asked her if she was aware of the cir-
38 cumstances. She was, but told me how she knew
39 these kinds of things never work, that kids never
40 follow through, and that she could have told me
41 beforehand that it wouldn't work. As I was about
42 to ask her if we could continue the conversation
43 the next day, she said, "All I know is that you han-
44 dled it badly. You really messed up!" *Click.* She
45 hung up.
46   As I drove home that night I passed my
47 supervising pastor's home. Since all the lights
48 were on, and since they were packing to move,
49 I stopped in to talk with him. His advice was
50 not to lose sleep over it. "There's nothing you
51 can do about it, that's just the way she is." I
52 talked at length that night with my wife, just to
53 work through my feelings.
54   The next day I stopped by Dorothy's place to
55 talk but nobody was home. I left my card. When I
56 saw her in church the next week I told her I had
57 stopped and would stop again after the new year.
58 I haven't been out there yet.

59 *Analysis*

60   I had mixed feelings. At first I was defensive.
61   This reaction was coming from a woman who is
62   living in the midst of one of the most dysfunc-
63   tional families in the congregation. Two years
64   ago she and her husband began to lead the
65   senior high youth and have slowly caused that
66   youth group to crumble. The kids have said
67   they won't come because of them. As for what
68   she said to me about communicating with
69   junior high kids—ten to thirteen youth usually
70   come to each meeting, and they are asking if
71   we can meet on a weekly basis, instead of every
72   other week. So my first feelings were defensive.

73 *Evaluation*

74   I decided I really needed to talk with her the
75   next day. Her reputation precedes her, so I know
76   I am not the only person to hear from her. I
77   didn't have a problem with her being angry with
78   me, but with the way she expressed it. She was
79   very controlling; she wouldn't give me a chance
80   to say anything. After saying what she wanted to
81   say, she hung up. I know I won't change her, but
82   I want to address her tactics somehow. I found it
83   most offensive and inappropriate.

84 *Theological Reflection*

85   In reflecting on this situation theologically
86   and in terms of biblical images, I remembered
87   the texts about people possessed by demons.
88   The woman seemed somehow possessed; yet
89   there is more to her than the demon possession.
90   I felt there must be some grace in the situation,

91 and some sense that the demons could be cast
92 out. I am also considering what this says about
93 ministry and especially about how I minister in
94 situations of anger and conflict.

REFLECTION ON THE PRESENTER'S MINISTRY EVOKED BY "THE WRATH OF MOM"

In reflecting on the presenter's effectiveness, members of this case group (interns and field education staff) commended David for his clarity about the woman's anger and the way she used it. They also noted the positive way he tried to work out his own feelings immediately with his supervisor and with his wife. They commended his desire to follow through with the angry mother, but suggested he first consider what her anger and blame means for him personally and as he understands himself as pastor. There was an important discussion about being pastoral and yet setting limits on what one will receive from a parishioner. They also encouraged David to deal with his own anger at the woman and at her misunderstandings of him and his role with the youth.

When the presenter came back into the discussion to offer his reflections, he expressed his own concern about the two sides of himself: the "nice side" and the "not so nice side," the second of which is "really hard for me." He then asked for more help on how he might approach the angry woman when he went to see her. The facilitator encouraged him to role-play the situation, with the facilitator taking the part of the woman. Part of the role-play follows:

Presenter: Dorothy, I want to continue the conversation we had on the phone after the Christmas party. First I want to acknowledge the fact that you were angry with me. I understand there are some issues that you were angry about, especially that I switched presents when it seemed that Dan's present was for someone in particular and I had given it to someone else. I was wondering if you could talk to me a bit more about how you were feeling then.

Facilitator: Well, we spent lots of money with a particular child in mind, and it's clear you hadn't thought about that possibility. If you had, you would have seen that sort of thing was going to happen. And I have to admit I'm really still very angry with you! So what is it you want from me now?

Presenter: I want to talk a bit about the end of the conversation when you hung up on me. I understand that you were angry with me. But it concerns me that you hung up on me without giving me a chance to talk.

Facilitator: Well, I was just too angry to talk any more. I'd said what I had to say.

Presenter: Well, with all due respect, Dorothy, I don't think that was a very appropriate way of dealing with it. By hanging up on me, you basically took a lot of control in the situation; you took everything away from me and didn't allow me anything. I would ask that the next time you're very angry with something I have done, that if you're at the point where you want to hang up, please say something and don't just hang up or not call. I'd be glad to talk to you about it later.

Facilitator: Let's stop the role play right there. What has David done well?

Mary: He's acknowledged where Dorothy was and has said to her that it is basically O.K. to be frustrated with somebody.

Betty: You were objective and clear about your own feelings without blowing up at her. You stated the situation clearly, but you didn't get angry physically or verbally at her. That's very positive.

Jay: Did you want to yell at her?

Presenter: No, I didn't.

Jay: That was good, to not yell.

Facilitator: Anything that you'd have encouraged him to do differently?

Mary: I would use "I" statements.

Presenter: I was aware that at the beginning I was not looking at you. Then all of a sudden I looked up at you.

Facilitator: And that was really helpful . . . I was more engaged and it was easier when you looked at me even though you were saying hard things. You took a lot of time to affirm that you had heard what Dorothy had to say and you understood that she was angry. I think that's valuable. But you needed to get through that more quickly and get to, "But I'm also concerned about your behavior."

Vicki: The tone of your voice will help set limits, and she will know that she has stepped beyond them.

Presenter: So, in talking to her, is there really no need to address the issue she raised?

Jane: I don't think the gift exchange is the issue.

Betty: That would be dealing with details.

Presenter: I don't know but that she's feeling as though no one hears her.

Betty: You could check that out.

Jane: You might tell her it's hard to hear when she's yelling.

Facilitator: In writing about "the shadow," Carl Jung says we take the stuff we don't like in ourselves and we project it out here on somebody else who is our shadow. For the "nice boy," the shadow may be the shouter. There may be some things you can learn about yourself by learning about Dorothy.

Betty: Your shadow may well have been hooked by her shouting. Like projection it is very helpful when you are conscious of it.

Facilitator: David, I want to ask you, again, as we wrap up, the question we asked you very early on: As you go back to talk to her, what's the purpose of that? What do you now understand yourself to be wanting to accomplish?

Presenter: First of all, I want to be very clear about my limits. Approaching her is going to make me work through the whole conversation before I go, and clarify what my limits are. I also want to create a sense of authority on my part. I want to claim some of that. I am in a situation where I have a certain kind of authority, but it's not like the senior pastor's; it's sort of the office, but the authority is of a lower office.

Facilitator: You're working on really important issues that have to do with who you are as a man and who you are as a pastor. And I want to applaud how hard you're working on that right now. It seems to me that you have done a significant piece of work and that you are much clearer at the end of the hour about what hooks you about this case, and about why you want to deal with that, and about what you hope will come out of that. Thanks for sharing with us.

CONCLUSION

In the course of listening to the participants discuss his case, of reflecting on what they have shared, and in engaging fully in the role play, David has come to some insights and ways of changing his behavior with the "wrathful mom." Furthermore, he is now in touch with what had hooked him emotionally in the exchange, and has begun to see how these things relate to his images of himself as a man and as a pastor. Reflections from the seminar group and his own self-reflections have aided his thinking considerably.

In his own theological reflection on the case, the presenter notes the image of people possessed by demons. He is conscious that one who is possessed, as the "wrathful mom" seemed to be in her interaction with him, is also made up of more elements than the demonic. The presenter seeks to name and confront the demons—not only in the angry mother, but also in himself. The image of demon possession is a useful one for understanding the content of this particular case.

For understanding the purpose of the reflection section of the process, however, the image of midwife seems more pertinent. A midwife aids at a birthing. She coaches, encourages, supports, affirms, cheers on the one who is in labor and who finally, it is hoped, gives birth and brings forth new life. The Hebrew midwives, lauded and remembered by name in the first chapter of Exodus, not only encouraged the birthing mother, but also stood up against unjust demands to destroy life. They are aiders and abetters of life.

What is more, they cannot control what is being brought to birth. Michael Williams writes of Shiphrah and Puah as knowing "that their participation in the birthing process is limited to assisting something that can and will take place on its own and in its own time." He goes on to describe friends as those "called to be midwives for whatever God is bringing to birth in our friends."[1]

The members of a case study group may be seen, during the time of reflecting on the presenter's ministry, as taking on the role of friendly midwives with the presenter. They can neither control what will happen to the presenter as a result of the case consultation nor predict how the presenter will proceed in his own ministry to continue the process brought to focus through the case. They can, however, befriend the presenter—both through supporting his growth and through speaking the truth in love. In the case process

---

1. Michael E. Williams, "The Midwives' Story: An Image of the Faithful Friend," *Weavings*, vol. 12, no. 3 (May-June 1992).

of this chapter, David was aided by his peers and seminary supervisors to come to new insights about his "nice guy" side, his repressed anger, and his sense of his own authority. Through their midwifery, the group left space for David to move toward birthing a new way of being with a difficult parishioner who had evoked his shadow side. In response, the presenter, David, was able to image some fresh manifestation of inner authority.

Chapter Seven

Futuring

A method for theological case study is the subject matter of this book. But the writers' goal is to encourage an attitude about, and an understanding of, ministry. We are committed to case study, for our students and for our own ministries, because it helps us see clearly the reflective component of ministry. Ministry is about faithful response to God, the communities with which we work and worship, and the women and men who make them up. To respond faithfully requires a theological process that illuminates: ourselves and what we bring to the ministry situation, the context in which the situation exists, and the ways that God's people have sought to understand and do the will of the Holy One. The practice of ministry simply cannot be separated from the practice of reflection. Those in ministry are called to be practical theologians, what Donald Schoen calls reflective practitioners.[1]

PRESENTER AS STORY-TELLER

The cases quoted, discussed, and analyzed in the preceding chapters are examples of stories out of the actual practice of ministry, brought to gatherings of colleagues and mentors for consultation. Through such

---

1. Donald Schoen, *The Reflective Practitioner* (New York: Basic Books, 1983).

consultation, further knowing and understanding may be revealed, leading to a different way of being and doing on the part of the presenter. In addition, we hope that, through case study, all participants will reflect on their own ministries with fresh eyes and ears, bringing to the surface new questions and coming to fresh understandings.

Earlier we suggested, at several points, that ministerial case studies are short stories, slices of life from the presenters' full complex of functions and relationships. As stories, cases are a way to research one's discipleship. They affirm that one's personal and professional life is as privileged as any other story to be read and interrogated. The presenter controls the presentation of his or her case story. Then the presenter hears how the story is perceived by others. In the end, the presenter has the chance for a final interpretative comment. This process confirms the presenter's authority over her own learning and growth. The story-telling approach to case writing, presenting, and reflecting validates presenters as learners, opens up a way for participants to learn, and honors personal experiences as sources of knowledge.

In writing, telling, hearing, reading, and reflecting on slices of personal biographies in the form of cases, it is possible to probe minds at work as they interact with one another. It is possible to get glimpses of how lives are being influenced by culture, history, theology, and experience, and how people make sense of human interaction. Story-telling or case stories permit voices to speak and minds to meet across time and space. As people speak out and enter into dialogue about themselves, case stories are a way of making new sense out of existence. Case writers and their colleagues use insights gained in case discussion to redirect the course of their personal and professional lives by changing their minds and ways of ministering.

The process works like this. As a casewriter, I purposely interrupt the daily flow of my life. I sit at my desk and open my ministry practice for review, just as though I had taken a book off the shelf, opened it, and begun to read the text. I let my history flow past the eyes of my mind. I watch for scenes that catch and stop my eye. I linger with each for a while. Through my fingertips on the computer keyboard or with pen in hand, I begin to tell a short story. I decide on the sequence of events that brings it alive. I discern a significant marker or turning point on which to elaborate. I examine one of these turning points from multiple perspectives for possible meanings. Paradoxically, as I give this short account of a segment of my ministry, I am both drawn more deeply into it and provided greater distance from it. I relive and analyze my practice of ministry at the same time.

I look for metaphors. They are links between what goes on in my mind, what happens around me, and the larger tradition of which I am a part. I may discover that my inner images of God or of myself or my ministry are incompatible with how others see God or me or my ministry. These openings motivate me to ask why. I learn from my own case. When I share my story through case presentation, other hearers and I together can use it to reflect on our lives, discover points of disjunction, and engage in new learnings. In telling stories about my ministry practice in case form, I take responsibility for the course of my life and my care for others.

GROUP PARTICIPANTS AS CRITICS

If the case presenter can be thought of as a storyteller, the participants may be thought of as literary critics. We do not mean "critic" in the popular sense of one who judges another's work as worthy or unworthy. Rather, these critics, out of their own experience and reflection, bring theory to bear on the story at hand in order that it might be seen more clearly. They help bring its structures and implications to light. The audience for this work is the case presenter, who has offered up a story out of the ministry setting to which she will return. And the "critics" are persons in ministry who will, in turn, offer up their case stories. These "literary critics" are most like a group of writers who regularly gather to hear and respond to one another's work in progress.

The peer reflection group is essential to the process of preparation for professional ministry as a structure of mediation between study in the library and classroom and ministry practice. It provides a forum in which those in ministry can engage in a conversation regarding the insights of personal experience, Christian traditions, and the disciplines of the social sciences and humanities. In this way, seminarians gain experience in how communities of faith are formed and sustained. As the demands of ministry are clarified, pluriform responses are explored and factors impinging on pastoral decision making are examined.

Case-based peer reflection groups are more than an important part of formal, or informal, theological education. By offering participants a continuing community that provides supportive fellowship, intellectual engagement about our practice of ministry, and regular accountability, case groups are a part of the responsible practice of ministry.

The peer reflection group provides the person in ministry with a community of trusted colleagues who offer one another both support and challenge in a setting of confidentiality. Our experience with students, with our peers, and in our own growth suggests that this collegial accountability is crucial to continuing professional development. Yet such accountability and support are too seldom experienced by those in professional ministry after their formal education or certification is accomplished. We bear witness to the growth-producing value of such groups for reflective practice out of our experience of offering up the stories of our lives in ministry for peer reflection as well as in guiding student reflection.

In some settings case groups have been fairly homogeneous, while others have experimented with varying degrees of diversity. It is clear that there are trade-offs to be made. Diversity increases the range of perspectives brought to bear on the case. Commonality tends to make it easier to build trust and arrive at shared understandings. As field educators, we seek to constitute the small groups, of eight to twelve members, with the diversity of age, race, nationality, and gender represented in the larger seminary population. Thus participants discover that pluralism carries benefits for the church. The existence of diverse experiences, beliefs, and theological formulations communicates the ultimate mystery of the inclusive God and the many forms that ministry takes in varied settings. Our goal is not to blend them all into one dominant form but to experiment with how to assess and coordinate forms.

If you are assembling your own peer reflection group, you will need to consider the degree of diversity in which you choose to engage. Whom do you wish to reach out to to include? Whose reflections do you seek to help you understand more fully your own ministry?

Using the analysis of styles of group life from the work of Evelyn Eaton Whitehead and James D. Whitehead, we suggest that peer groups function somewhere on a continuum between primary groups and formal organizations.[2]

They will exhibit some characteristics found in both these styles, but they are unique. As in primary groups, like families, emotional ties develop and communication is face-to-face. Deep personal sharing can occur. Members perform support functions. On the other hand, members are also united by their engagement in ministry based in a commitment to traditions and organizations wider than individual histories and personal friendships. Members perform critical feedback functions in order to promote personal and professional effectiveness in the wider arenas of ministry.

Participants present and respond to cases, engage in supervision, and share resources that have served to quicken their sense of the Spirit at work in their lives, in order that they will be enriched in their practice of ministry. We expect that those in formal training for ministry will find support from the peer groups which encourage them to seek ways to make case reflection a continuing part of their ministry. We offer our experience with case study to informal groups learning about their shared ministries, as well as to more formal groups of practitioners and supervisors, lay and ordained, in seminaries, churches, hospitals, and other settings.

Case groups provide safe spaces in which we can try out new roles, speak in new languages, test new thoughts, and repeatedly revise those roles, languages,

---

2. *Community of Faith: Models and Strategies for Developing Christian Communities* (New York: Seabury Press, 1982).

and thoughts that get in the way of growth and effective ministry. We teach one another how to stop, look, and listen like the watcher stationed on the ramparts awaiting God's reply to the question, "How long shall I cry for help?" (Hab. 1:2). Together we learn how to hear with ears attentive to nuance, to metaphor, to potentially healthful change. Together we learn how to quiet the voices that harm and denigrate people and how to speak in voices that support and encourage.

THEOLOGICAL REFLECTION UNDERGIRDED BY SCRIPTURE

We assume, as Christians, that scripture makes a claim on us and our ministries. Thus a part of the theological task is to consider how my story converses with The Story. In writing this book, the authors have carried on a conversation between our experience of casework in ministry and our experience of the biblical stories. At times cases or questions about how to reflect on cases have called up scripture. At other times returning to favorite texts has cast new light on our thinking about case reflection as ministry.

Nathan confronting King David (2 Sam. 12:1-7*a*) helped us to understand the way that our own cases bring to light issues in our ministries we haven't been aware of, and sometimes don't want to be confronted by. The story of the bent-over woman and the bent-over man (Luke 13:10-17) reminds us of how liberating it is to be seen and known by One who believes we can be healed and be different in our reengagement of the world. Jesus' question to blind Bartimaeus (Mark 10:46-52) reminds us of the presenter's own authority in reflecting on her ministry. As participants, we join Jesus in asking, "What would you have [us] do for you?" The parable of the sower (Matt. 13:1-9) helps us understand that as participants we don't need to see and say everything perfectly, and as presenters we don't have to take in everything the participants offer. Seed is scattered, and from it God calls forth a harvest. The woman who anoints Jesus (Matt. 26:6-13) suggests something of how personal, even intimate, case reflection can be. Recognizing what is precious in another, we pour out what insight we have. We are tempted to believe that it will not be sufficient, but in interacting with the story of the feeding of the 5,000 (Matt. 14:13-21), we are reminded of how many times God has blessed what we have to offer and made it enough. The process of case sharing, rich though it can be, is not easy. But the image of the midwives of Israel (Exod. 1:8-22) points us to our courageous peers, who bear us up, encouraging us in the process of giving birth to new understandings of ourselves and our ministries.

The stories in scripture of God's faithfulness are powerful sources to undergird ministry. But the Christian tradition is dynamic. The Spirit is active in the action of our contemporaries as well as in the past. Our thinking about the nature of ministry and the process of reflection in ministry has been shaped by our peers and students, like those whose cases appear here. They have made themselves vulnerable by offering up their ministries for reflection.

In the busyness of serving, time needs to be set aside for contemplation. In case presentation, as in every other aspect of ministry, there is potential for theological reflection. There is a depth that comes with the more disciplined practice that ministry demands. What is the nature of this serving called ministry? What do our actions suggest about who God is, what the human condition is, and how Good News is shared?

112

CASE STUDY FOR LIFELONG LEARNING

Many of those who use this book will have had formal theological education or be at work obtaining a theological education. But we believe that formation for ministry is a lifelong quest. Because our experience of God, our self-understandings, and our relationship to the communities we are called to serve are not static, our own religious education must always be in process.

The case study process, as we have described it and as we are using it, provides continuing support and accountability within ministry. It is our hope that seminary students, having discovered the benefits of case study, will establish support groups in their places of ministry where cases will continue to aid their self-reflection and ministry practice.

For all of us in ministry, case study is one method of engaging in the reflective practice required by our calling. Ministry requires more than refinement of skill. God's people make sense of life by connecting inner visions of God with action in the world. Ministry is rooted in continuing self-reflection and theological focus, as well as in keen analysis of the context and needs of those with whom we minister. When inner and outer realities do not match, new or revised languages, images, and symbols are needed to make vital connections, to celebrate fresh meaning in life. Faith is challenged. In working through to new connections, faith can be deepened and strengthened. Case study is thus offered as a tool for deepening the interpretative skills that undergird faithful ministry.

An experienced supervisor sees the issues of his case revealed in clearer form through the clarifying questions of his peers. Through a case about his first funeral, a new pastor offers participants in a case group opportunity to reflect on and learn from their own awkwardness early in their ministries. A seminarian serving in a culture different from her original one and in a case group comprising women from diverse ethnic groups is opened to considering a variety of perspectives on the giving and receiving of monetary gifts. A case group grapples with theological reflection around issues of authority between an intern and her supervisor. A youth pastor enters into further learning about projection and receives encouragement to honor his own anger and his own limits. All of the persons involved in the cases presented here are becoming constructive knowers, tapping a deeper wisdom that leads them to more effective ministry.

The particular method of case study described here is but one approach we have found to be extremely beneficial for seminarians, pastors, Christian educators, and field education staff supervisors. We commend it to you for your consideration, in the hope that you will receive it as an open invitation to develop your own methods, models, and metaphors within case reflection. At the end of the case process the presenter goes back into the ministry setting. The facilitator's last act is to ask the presenter what has been helpful in the process, what new insights have been gained, and how the presenter will reengage the situation. The reader is now faced with the same questions. You are the one who must decide what has been helpful to you in reading this book. How has it quickened your understanding of the task of the practical theologian—which you share with all those in ministry? What changes in your practice will you make as a result of this process of reflection?

Appendix One

Writing the Case

A s the case presenter, it is your task to bring a focused, written account of an incident in your ministry about which you seek the counsel of your peers. Guidelines and an outline for writing the case follow:

GUIDELINES:

1) *The case is about you and your ministry.* It involves an actual incident in which you were involved as a minister with some responsibility for the outcome. It is not a hypothetical situation, or a situation in which you were simply an observer. Remember, the goal is for your peers to be able to consult with you. Write in the first person, reporting things as you saw them. It is helpful to describe emotional tone, body language, and setting, for these also are part of your lived experience.

2) *The case is confidential.* The group should have a covenant of confidentiality of which the facilitator can remind them. You can point to this covenant by withholding identifications that are not needed. Use initials or fictitious names (e.g., Ms. A, "Mr. Brown," Church X). If you reveal the names, or the context makes identities clear, but you wish the information to be confidential within the group, write at the top: "CONFIDENTIAL: for seminar use only." Collecting

the copies of the case at the end of the session to be disposed of discreetly is another way to remind the group of the importance of confidentiality.

3) *The written case should be brief.* The case report is to be no longer than what can be written on both sides of a single sheet of paper. Part of the discipline is to learn what can be condensed into this limited space. This requires you to identify the critical information. Lines should be numbered for easy reference.

4) *The case is a limited slice of ministry.* It is not a general "issue" or "problem," such as how to deal with difficult parishioners, but an incident in your ministry. The reflection will be on this specific incident. Provide only the background that you believe is necessary to understand the incident. Try to tell the story, and your response to it, in a clear, orderly progression, because this will assist your peers in reflecting on it with you.

A Model for Ministerial Case Writing

Case study brings together a *presenter* who has agreed to share in writing a critical incident from his or her practice of ministry for mutual confidential reflection with a group of peer *participants* under the direction of a *facilitator.* What follows is one model of case writing.

The case has five parts, which are to be distinguished clearly. They need not be equal in length, but each of the parts must be included.

1. *Background:* Give enough information to set the event in a context: what you had in mind, what you hoped or feared would happen, when and how you became aware of or involved in the event, what pressures and persons precipitated and shaped the event.

2. *Description:* Tell what happened and what you did. Report the event, including as much detail as possible in the limited space.

3. *Analysis:* Identify issues and relationships, with special attention to changes and resistance to change. Try to answer the question, What's going on here?

4. *Evaluation:* This is your estimate of your own effectiveness in the event. Did you do what you set out to do? Did you function effectively? If so, why so? If not, why not? What factors or forces emerged that you did not anticipate? What questions might the group discuss that would be most helpful to you?

5. *Theological reflection:* Include the biblical and theological themes which emerge in this situation (e.g., faith, guilt, alienation, reconciliation, justice, law, grace, sin, redemption, creation, incarnation, suffering, resurrection). Be specific about where you see evidence of them. Where is the activity of God in this situation?

2. *Description.* Tell what happened and what you did. Report the event, including as much detail as possible in the limited space.

3. *Analysis.* Identify issues and relationships, with special attention to changes and resistance to change. Try to answer the question, What's going on here?

4. *Evaluation.* This is your estimate of your own effectiveness in the event. Did you do what you set out to do? Did you function effectively? If so, why? If not, why not? What factors or forces emerged that you did not anticipate? What questions might the group discuss that would be most helpful to you?

5. *Theological reflection.* Include the biblical and theological themes which emerge in this situation (e.g. faith, guilt, alienation, reconciliation, justice, law, grace, sin, redemption, creation, incarnation, suffering, resurrection). Be specific about where you see evidence of their... Where is the activity of God in this situation?

Facilitating a Case

Here are some suggestions for facilitating the ministerial case study. They are followed by a brief outline of the recommended process and some examples of specific guiding questions to aid your facilitation of the case. Case facilitation can be done effectively in a number of ways. A personal life of faith and spiritual discipline, along with basic helping skills of attending, listening, and responding are the facilitator's primary tools.

GUIDELINES FOR FACILITATING

1) *Set up the room.* You want to put people at ease and relate them to one another. Placing chairs in a circle is a good way to do this. Try to maximize eye contact. Take time for introductions and checking in.

2) *Be clear where you are going.* Be sure that the presenter and the participants are clear how you will proceed so that there are not surprises for them. Tell the presenter when she or he will be invited to speak, and when to be a silent observer.

3) *Tend to the clock.* Either watch the clock yourself, or assign a participant to do this. Make sure that the group gets through the entire case process. Be sensitive to the point at which closure must occur.

4) *Encourage participation.* Your role is to facilitate the participants' conversation. Allow participants to ask their own questions; be open to new insights. Be supportive of "lone voices" and encourage shy persons.

5) *Allow conflict.* When conflict arises, invite participants into direct dialogue. Be clear, however, that the focus of discussion is the presenter's case, not a difference of opinion among participants.

6) *Encourage sensitivity to other perspectives.* Help the group build listening skills, ask for clarification, give feedback, and solicit information where it is needed. Honor contributions, attempting to balance the group's needs with the presenter's stated goals.

7) *Value the authority of personal experience.* Things finally mean to us what we make of them. This is especially clear when you invite the presenter to report what has been helpful to him or her.

8) *Ground the discussion in the facts of the case.* Where participants seem to wander, or to reinterpret the case in light of their own agendas, ask them to relate their remarks to the case as presented.

9) *Don't be afraid of:* silences, conflict, or humor.

10) *Enjoy yourself!*

OUTLINE FOR CASE PRESENTATION AND DISCUSSION

Following is a simple outline of the recommended case process. It may be duplicated and shared with the group so that they can see clearly where the process is going.

Case Presentation

1) *Presenting the Case Aloud.* Participants follow along on their written copy noting questions or insights as the presenter reads the case.

2) *Clarifying the Information.* Here our goal is not analysis or interpretation, but understanding the case as the presenter represents it. Our central question is, Do we understand the presenter's description of what happened?

3) *Sharing Personal Wisdom.* Here our goal is to connect the case and presenter to the lived experience of the other participants and to become aware of the feelings and images each of us brings to the case.

4) *Pooling Professional and Educational Wisdom.* Here participants have the chance to offer the presenter the fruits of their training in the social sciences, psychology, literature, science, business, and so on.

5) *Claiming the Wisdom of the People of God.* Questions of theology and spirit inform the entire case process, but here they are made explicit.

6) *Reflecting on the Presenter's Ministry.*
   a) Action to date. The group turns its attention to reflection on the performance of the presenter-minister.
   b) Action in the future. Having reflected on the act of ministry, we ask, What implications are to be drawn for ministry in the future?

7) *Evaluating the Process.* The presenter is asked, What has been most helpful? What learnings have been gleaned?

121

POT-STIRRING QUESTIONS

What follows is an amplified list of questions that may be helpful to you in leading a group through the process. Our preference is to follow the questions that emerge from the group, but these can serve as "pot stirrers." These questions for facilitators to consider are not unique to the authors. They draw on the experience of previous field educators at Garrett-Evangelical as well as conversation with field educators from a number of seminaries about what has worked for them.

Don't use this as a checklist in your group; it is offered to inform the facilitator's preparatory reflection. Do draw on your own wisdom, as well as your understanding of the needs and abilities of the presenter and participants in processing a case. It is evident from the range of models available to us that case facilitation can be conducted effectively in a number of different ways.

The facilitator needs to listen especially for the religiously centered events, which may or may not be described in the images and vocabulary of the faith community, and help the presenter and participants to address them theologically.

1. Presenting the Case Aloud

Participants follow along on their written copy noting any questions or insights that emerge as the presenter reads through the case. The facilitator may wish to assign particular participants to pay attention to specific issues, such as: nonverbal communication, a sense of direction or movement, conflict, avoidance or resistance, intimacy or aloofness, self-awareness of the presenter, and so forth.

2. Clarifying the Information

Here our goal is *not* analysis or interpretation, but understanding the case as the presenter represents it.

- What is unclear?
- Do you understand the relationships and events of the case?
- How are the relationships ordered?
- What feelings did the presenter experience at the time? now?
- What did she or he fear?
- Where did she or he feel competent?
- What is the degree of emotional, imaginative, and intellectual intensity?
- Are the feelings and attitudes of others in the case clear?
- What theological or spiritual issues are overtly raised in the case?
- On what issue or issues is the presenter most needing the group's consultation?

Don't preach, judge, or try to solve problems. After the group has raised its questions, invite the presenter to offer any further clarification he or she feels is needed.

3. Sharing Personal Wisdom

Here our goal is to connect the case and presenter to the lived experience of the other participants and to become aware of what each of us brings to the case.

- What feelings does the case evoke in the participants?

- When have you been in a similar situation, known similar people, faced similar issues?
- What word or image captures the story?
- With what pain or joy in the participants' lives does this case connect?

4. Pooling Professional and Educational Wisdom

We bring our professional and educational histories, as well as our personal wisdom and experience, to bear on the case. Remind the group of their wisdom with questions appropriate to their background.

- What insights from your educational or work experience can you offer the presenter?
- What assumptions about human nature are at work in this case and our response to the case?
- What social or cultural forces are at work?
- Do questions of social structure, race, class, gender, or power relationships help us understand this case?
- What do we know about individual psychic development, family or group systems, or faith development that might inform this case?
- If the case were a literary text or film, what critical tools would help us understand it? how?
- How is this a universal human experience?
- What does our culture say about this experience? Are we aware of wisdom from other cultures?

5. Claiming the Wisdom of the People of God

Questions of theology and spirit inform the entire case process, but here they are made explicit. The facilitator needs to choose an approach appropriate to the facilitator's gifts, the specifics of the case, and the experience of the group.

Here are some possible questions or areas that focus the "Wisdom of the People of God":

• How have God's people responded to similar situations in other times and places? What do those responses suggest about the nature of ministry?
• (If the participants are students) How does your course work and reading speak to this case?
• What biblical story, image, or symbol comes to mind that illuminates or is evoked by this case?
• What doctrine of the church (ecclesiology) is portrayed?
• A Wesleyan approach (which might be fleshed out with some of the questions that follow) would test whether our theological reflection is:
    —revealed in Scripture
    —illumined by tradition
    —brought alive in personal experience
    —confirmed by reason.
• What image or images of God and humanity are expressed in the case? What is the nature, power, and limit of each? Where are these images of God and persons supported or confronted or challenged by scripture or church tradition? Where is (or what kind of) God (is) at work?
• What is the "Work of Christ" here?
• Where (how) is the Holy Spirit at work?
• H. Richard Niebuhr's categories in *Christ and Culture* might lead you to explore whether in this case the relationship of "Christ and culture" is viewed by those in the case as being:
    —Christ of Culture
    —Christ Against Culture

125

—Christ Above Culture
—Christ and Culture in Paradox
—Christ the Transformer of Culture

How do assumptions about the relationship of Christ and culture shape the expectations of the presenter and others in this case about what constitutes appropriate ministry in this situation?[1]

• Identify the theological concepts operative in the case, such as:[2]

New Jerusalem/	Indwelling	Creation
Kingdom	Honesty	Sacrifice
Conscience	Sin	Grace
Church	Peace	Servant/Service
Redemption	Love	Revelation
Faith	Covenant	Vocation
Justice	Compassion	Freedom
Ministry	Renewal	Discernment
Incarnation	Prophecy	Obedience
Celebration	Creator	Savior
Authority	Spirit	

Choose one of the concepts identified by the participants to pursue. What is it about this concept that energizes, confronts, criticizes, or confirms this case?

• What is the "lived theology" of the case? What story or stories are being lived out? What assumptions about God and humanity, good and evil, are reflected here?

1. H. Richard Niebuhr, *Christ and Culture* (New York: Harper and Row, 1951).
2. This list of concepts is based on the "Franciscan Method" in the *Ministry I Handbook* of Catholic Theological Union, Chicago, Ill., p. 30.

6. Reflecting on the Presenter's Ministry

Only at the end of a thorough reflection on the case do we indicate our judgment about the presenter's gifts and graces and offer suggestions for how the presenter might reengage the ministry situation.

A. *Action to date.* In light of the pooling of wisdom about the case, and what it means to the group, reflect on the performance of the presenter.

- What sort of ministry was this (priest, prophet, governor, shepherd, teacher, mentor, companion, friend, guide, servant)?
- What worked well? what didn't?
- What seemed connected to the needs and concerns of the person ministered to?
- What seemed connected to the needs and concerns of the presenter?

B. *Action in the future.* Having looked at the act of ministry and reflected on it, ask what implications can be drawn for ministry in the future.

- What is our future hope for this situation in ministry?
- How may the presenter continue in ministry in this situation?
- What counsel does the group offer?
- How might the group be supportive of the presenter in his or her growth in ministry?
- What issues in the case call forth the prayers of the presenter and the group? What do we pray for? why? What does this tell us about the God we pray to?

- Assess the options for ministry, those exercised and those which are still possible. Where the group members offer contradictory advice, ask the question: How would or would not each option affirm or change the situation in the light of the gospel?

7. Evaluating the Process

Having listened at some length to the reflection of peers, the presenter is offered a chance to share his or her evaluation of how the case process has gone. Guiding questions might include:

- How do you feel about your colleagues' comments and reflections? Where were they supportive; where did you feel attacked?
- What learnings have been gleaned?
- Are there misunderstandings you want to clarify?
- What has been most helpful?

Conclude by thanking the presenter and the participants. Have the presenter collect copies of the case to preserve confidentiality.

Appendix Three

Alternative Settings

Throughout this book it has been argued that case reflection has the potential to be used fruitfully throughout a lifetime of ministry. The authors find that case reflection on our own work continues to shape and inform our understandings of ourselves as persons, and as persons in ministry. "William's Case: A Conflict of Backgrounds," which illustrates and informs chapter 2, demonstrates that others with many years of experience also find this process helpful. Yet we recognize that most of the cases used in the preceding chapters confirm that our experience with case reflection is shaped, for the most part, by our work with persons in the midst of formal theological training.

Eager to clarify how our experience matches or contrasts with that of others who minister in different settings, we asked three persons to read the manuscript and reflect on the possibility of its application in their setting for ministry. George Fitchett, an experienced Clinical Pastoral Education supervisor, is Director of Research and Spiritual Assessment at Rush-Presbyterian-St. Luke's Medical Center in Chicago. Donald Guest is past president of the Northern Illinois Chapter of Black Methodists for Church Renewal and pastor of Gammon United Methodist Church in Chicago. Diane Olson is a gifted Christian educator who serves as

Diaconal Minister at Trinity United Methodist Church in Wilmette, Illinois. Their reflections follow:

SHARED WISDOM IN CLINICAL PASTORAL EDUCATION

George Fitchett

The case study method described here is a superb instrument to promote learning and growth in ministry. In this text the authors have created an excellent resource for understanding and using this instrument. Illustrating each stage in the discussion with an actual case makes the model very tangible. The selection of a biblical text and theological image for each stage of the case study process also is one of the superior features of this work. By including these biblical stories, the authors model theological reflection even as they write about how to teach it.

A significant number of the authors' aims, assumptions, and methods about case study are shared by Clinical Pastoral Education (CPE) supervisors. The goal of both case study and CPE is to increase ministerial effectiveness. We share an understanding that this goal is both part of preparation for ministry and a lifelong task. We share an understanding of the importance of the person of the minister, his or her strengths and growing edges, as a key factor in ministerial effectiveness. We share a view of all believers, and not just pastors, as participants in ministry and therefore as persons who could contribute to and benefit from case study.

Both case study and CPE are reflection on the actual, not imagined or observed, practice of ministry. Both methods are designed to facilitate the transformation of classroom learning and personal spiritual maturity into competence as a pastor. The sections of the case study process summarize the specific areas which both case study and CPE hold to be relevant in building ministerial competence. These include awareness of one's emotional and interpersonal patterns and the way they come into play in ministry, ability to think about the theological aspects of concrete situations in life, and the ability to conceive and carry out an effective plan for ministry.

Both case study and CPE believe that the learning process begins as the student takes time to write down the details of a case and begins to reflect on the case. Case study and CPE both see a group of learners as the ideal method for this kind of education. To return to one of the authors' biblical metaphors, Jesus' feeding of the five thousand, by sharing from their own gifts, peers in the learning group can help multiply the wisdom available to the presenter and to all the members of the study group.

There are also some differences between case study and CPE. The authors' model for case study ensures a breadth of analysis for each case presented. For each case, personal wisdom, professional wisdom, theological reflection, and practical application are all considered. Many CPE verbatim or case study outlines will include all these elements, but frequently the actual discussion of the case focuses in greater depth on one or two elements. In CPE there is more emphasis on following the issues that emerge in the case discussion than in covering all the important facets of the case. The breadth of analysis and reflection achieved in one seminar by the authors' model for case study often requires several sessions in CPE.

Although CPE uses a variety of tools for written reporting and reflection on ministry, including case studies, the verbatim is probably the most widely used tool. Verbatims, like case studies, often include background, analysis, evaluation, and theological reflection. But unlike the case study, a verbatim report of a ministerial encounter replaces the summarized description. What difference does this make? Focusing on the verbatim account of a conversation makes one very conscious of the details of the words, tone, gesture, and silence that form our communication with one another. The verbatim is an excellent tool with which to study how empathetic distance or connection are created with others. After writing one or two verbatims, beginners in ministry usually go through a period in which they are very self-conscious about their pastoral conversations and body language. More confident practitioners value the verbatim for the way it discloses the rich nuances of relationships and communication.

By drawing attention to the details of communication and relationships, the use of the verbatim in CPE encourages reflection on the person and skills of the minister and the needs of the person being cared for. Theological reflection can be based on verbatims, but the summarized description of an incident in ministry lends itself well to stepping back and thinking about the theological issues in a case.

Another difference between case study and CPE is the role of the peer group. In both models there is sensitivity to establishing a trusting and supportive learning community. However, in case study the relationships among the group members do not become a subject for discussion. In almost every CPE program, there is time for the group members to discuss their relations with one another and with the supervisor. The extent to which this is emphasized varies from group to group and supervisor to supervisor.

The differences between case study and CPE notwithstanding, there are many similarities. Many CPE supervisors will find it easy and enjoyable to apply this model in their programs. It may be particularly useful for the growing parish-based CPE programs. I think it could also be modified for use in professional peer reviews. I am sure that it has a lot to offer for experienced persons in ministry. The group support and consultation which are part of the model might be important resources in addressing that portion of clergy misconduct which stems from isolation and stress.

CASE REFLECTION FOR PARISH PASTORS

Donald F. Guest

It is an unfortunate reality that few pastors come together on a regular basis to reflect on their ministry. Pastors certainly "feel themselves to be in lonely and highly individualized professions." This has led to adverse effects including early "burnout" and low morale. Except for the occasional lectionary group, most pastors tend to encounter one another in bureaucratic and highly politicized meetings, which do not readily lend themselves to theological reflection. When clergy do come together for informal gatherings, time is usually at a premium. Much of this time is spent in what our authors have referred to as "checking in." Such unstructured "clergy catharsis" demonstrates that many of us are trying to do alone what God has intended to be the work of the larger community that D. Elton Trueblood referred to as "The Company of the Committed." We suffer needlessly. The possibility of creatively, collectively, and efficiently sharing "the load" is right in front of us. Following are a few suggestions

133

that I hope will assist my clergy sisters and brothers in using the content of this book to overcome their isolation and together enhance their ministries and strengthen their faith.

Begin by thinking small. By starting with a large group such as a district or synod meeting, one will ensure that the process never gets off the ground. If you are already involved in a lectionary study group, you might think about using this book as a source of study. Before actually working on a case written by a member of your group, it might prove helpful for the study group to examine the sample cases and the connecting biblical images presented for each of the steps in the case study method. The group should make its own decisions as to how these images are helpful and how other images might also be helpful in adapting the case study method to their needs.

For example, chapter 2 mentions a variant style. Letting the participants share connections in their lives while the presenter is still in the process of sharing the case with the group can reduce the anxiety of "holding that thought and losing it," as other salient connections displace it in the process. In my own community of African American clergy, this variant method will find greater acceptance. It is important to work with the model and adapt it for the special needs of your particular clergy grouping.

When reviewing the issue of confidentiality, honest discussion is needed among the clergy involved. A breach of confidentiality is serious for any case group. This issue becomes even more problematic for pastors, where a breach of confidentiality can mean the permanent loss of a parishioner's trust. By changing names, omitting specific contexts, and altering stated relationships we can re-create the conversation and revisit the incident in ministry without betraying details that allow others to make needless connections.

Retelling a case using broad narrative strokes frees us to think more broadly about the issues raised. At the same time, pastors should be encouraged to reproduce the actual spoken words of persons to the best of their ability. The actual spoken words protect the experienced pastor from a tendency to blend previous ministry experiences with the one intended to be shared. The strength of the authors' approach is that it deals with actual, not idealized, cases. Care should be taken to prevent the group from losing the "essentials" of a given case. The feedback we give and the evaluation of the presenter's ministry are tools he or she can use to better conduct his or her own ministry. If the feedback is to be effective, it must be a response to the spirit of that person's ministry. It is through our understanding of the spirit of one another's ministry that we can begin to assess the ways in which we are and are not drawing from our ultimate strength.

For those who have no lectionary study group, I strongly urge starting with a group of at least three or four. This is the minimum number of persons who can effectively participate in the process. Although it is possible for two persons to reflect structurally on an incident of ministry for each other, there are obvious deficiencies. It becomes harder to allow the presenter the luxury of being only a listener through most of the process, and it thus denies the presenter the chance to fully take in others' responses before responding. At least two respondents *and* a facilitator bring greater clarity and integrity to the process. Given the real (though unconfessed) competitive nature of pastors, it is imperative that some amount of trust be established. This cannot take place with a large group of pastors. A small group should covenant to read this book thoroughly before coming together. After reading the material, they should come together to decide whom they might want to add to the initial group. After this decision has been made, a careful study of the case study method should commence. If there does not seem to be a mutually agreed on time when you can meet free of all distractions, you might want to consider using one of your two "off days." Having worked extensively with the case study method, I commend it to you as a tool for discovering yourself and your ministry anew.

CHRISTIAN EDUCATION AND CASE STUDY METHOD

Diane C. Olson

The process of reflecting on ministry issues provides many opportunities for persons in the field of Christian education. Even the title of the book, "Shared Wisdom," implies two of the foundations of Christian education: "Wisdom" indicates previous learning, and "shared" implies learning for both facilitator and participant, a mutuality of learning leading to wisdom. Thus, the process outlined in this book holds great promise as a technique for nonhierarchical exploration of issues facing Christian educators. Case study is actually an approach to Christian education. Reflection facilitates knowledge, particularly reflection in dialogue with one another.

Examples of how Christian educators can use this case study process include teacher training sessions, Christian educator fellowship or support groups, and lay or peer reflection groups. Every Christian educator will recognize others in which this method would be useful. The lay group may meet on a regular basis and is chosen by the Christian educator, who may meet with the group to purposely reflect on ministry issues. Such a group helps the educator see incidents and issues in her own work through new lenses, providing creative alternatives for future ministry.

The teacher training sessions and fellowship and support groups can serve as settings for case study reflection because the participants share common goals of dedication to the process of education and to students, and, at the same time, have diverse and unique perspectives on issues. There may be a wide range of theological opinion and biblical knowledge, and experience in the field. The probability is high that these two settings would use reflection on cases as only part of their agendas, leaving time for business, announcements, and so on. In other words, these two kinds of groups would have a "life" not limited to reflection, which would allow for the development of relationships, trust, and collegiality. However, the occasional use of the case study method in these two settings, and the nearly exclusive use in the lay or peer reflection group, would offer many opportunities for growth of the participants in all three settings.

Many different kinds of issues could be addressed through the case study method in all three settings. Ministry issues, such as decision making, conflict resolution, cultural differences, and more are discussed in this book. One can include staff relationships, interdenominational concerns, administrative skills, and theological differences among the ministry issues. Pastoral care issues blend with the other ministry issues, but they are listed here separately because of the variety of pastoral care issues in the educational arena. Participants in a "shared wisdom" reflection session will identify pastoral care issues ranging from parenting to aging to interpersonal skills. Part of the excitement of using this approach is the variety of issues identified, and the recognition that the facilitator will not be able to identify all of them before the case is presented!

Another area where the "Shared Wisdom" approach has great value for Christian educators is in the development of skill. The participants will learn new skills, methods, and facts from the shared experiences of the group. An example important to Christian education may be a knowledge of developmental characteristics, which could be shared by one participant and consequently brought into the experience of the whole group.

New skills are learned as they are shared. The confidence of both participants and facilitator is increased as they gain skills in dealing with difficult situations, and as they reflect on the actions of others in these situations. Further, there is a greater ability to identify theological issues and "use" biblical comparisons. This ensures the integration of the Story of our faith into human experience in new ways.

Of course, there are many situations within the work of the Christian educator that allow for such integration, but the structure presented in this book provides experiences where engagement, safety, and purpose are offered. It is engaging, because it allows for differences among people, drawing them in where their own experiences meet the stories of others. It is safe, because participants know what to expect and the sharing creates trust. It has purpose and direction, but provides the chance to make comparisons and bring in related experience without deviating from the purpose.

The use of the case reflection method by Christian educators helps us to name our experiences, relate them to biblical and theological understandings, and thus increase our own understanding of God's work among us. As our understanding grows, we can become more focused in our own practice of ministry.

• • •

The authors are grateful to these colleagues for their words of praise, and for their thoughtful consideration of how case reflection is, or could be, used in their settings for ministry. We hope that their reflections will encourage others with long experience in ministry to seek out peers with whom they can reflect on the meanings and effects of their ministries.

Appendix Four

Resources for Use in Further Study

Browning, Don S. *Practical Theology: The Emerging Field in Theology, Church, and World.* San Francisco: Harper and Row, 1983.

The authors of this collection of essays, scholars who teach in a variety of fields, set the practice of ministry within its community surroundings and the church's mission in the world. They offer historical and foundational perspectives for rethinking the intersection between theology and theory, especially in the practice of pastoral care, teaching, and religious education. Case studies are included. Browning is Alexander Campbell Professor of Religion and Psychological Studies at the Divinity School of the University of Chicago.

Coll, Regina. *Supervision of Ministry Students.* Collegeville, Minn.: The Order of St. Benedict, 1992.

This director of field education in the theology department of the University of Notre Dame offers examples, patterns, and models of theological reflection as the central core of the work that supervisors and ministry students do together. From within a theoretical framework of viewing supervision as both education and ministry, the author has created a helpful "hands-on" manual.

Mudge, Lewis S., and James N. Poling, eds. *Formation and Reflection: The Promise of Practical Theology*. Philadelphia: Fortress Press, 1987.

Mudge, Dean of the Seminary and Professor of Theology at San Francisco Theological Seminary, and Poling, Professor of Practical Theology at Colgate Rochester Divinity School, have brought together essays aimed at exploring the relationship between formation of Christian identity and reflection by the people of God on the process.

Patton, John. *From Ministry to Theology: Pastoral Action and Reflection*. Nashville: Abingdon Press, 1990.

This professor of pastoral theology at Columbia Theological Seminary draws on the insights and vignettes of experiences of clinical pastoral education supervisors and students to explore the connections between the practice of ministry and Christian theology, with a focus more on the process than results and how acting affects thinking. Patton includes laity among those who are accountable for pastoral caregiving.

Whitehead, James D., and Evelyn Eaton Whitehead. *Method in Ministry: Theological Reflection and Christian Ministry*. Minneapolis: Winston Press, 1980.

The authors, noted for their work in the area of continuing education in ministry, demonstrate the use of a method of theological reflection in ministry that makes use of three sources—Christian tradition, experience of the community of faith, and the resources of culture—in three moves, attending, asserting, and decision making. Case studies are included. This book has become a classic in the field.